Seasons of the Fae

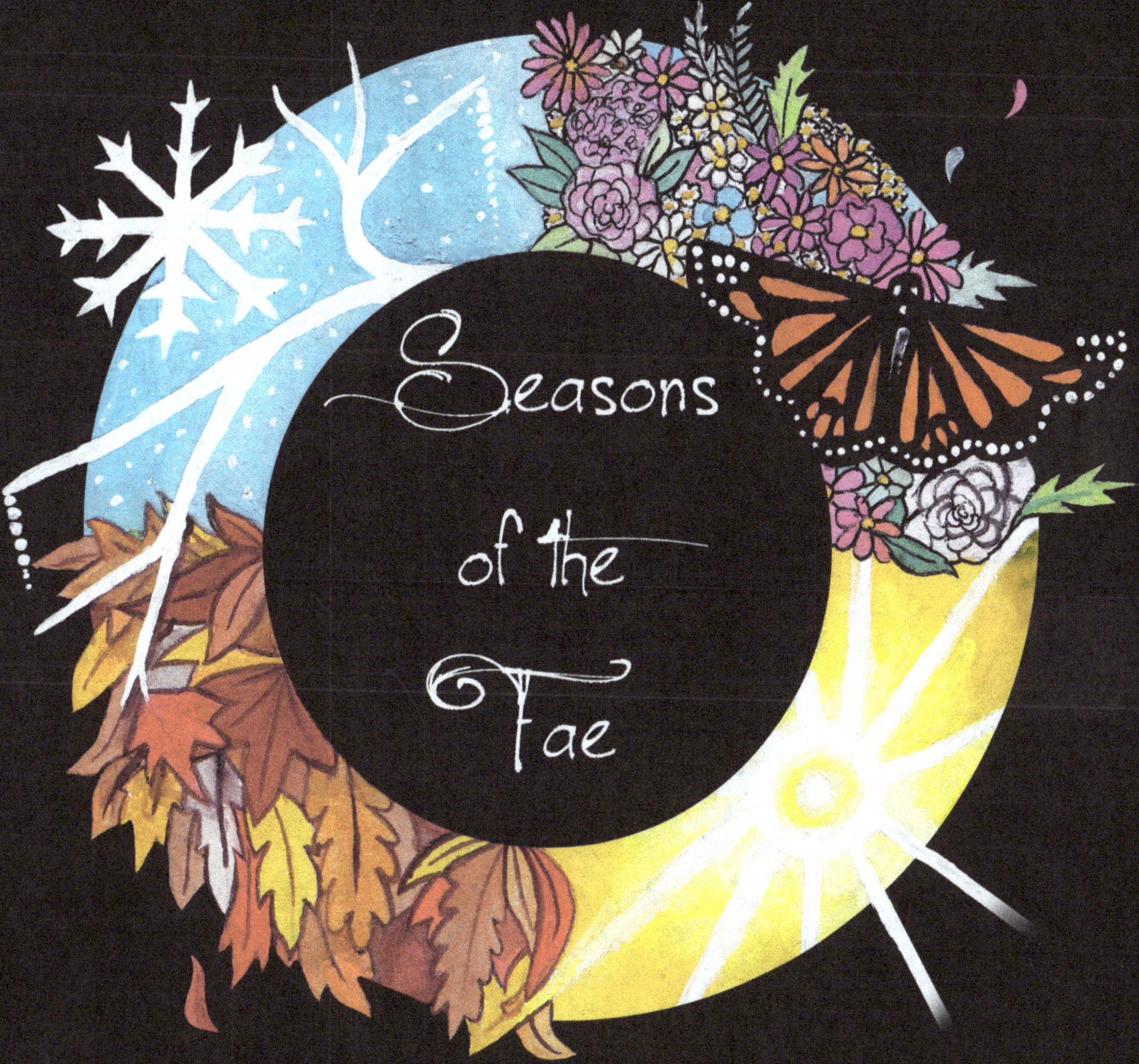

Sabrina RG Raven

Published by Ouroborus Book Services
www.ouroborusbooks.com

Art by Sabrina RG Raven
www.sabrinargraven.com

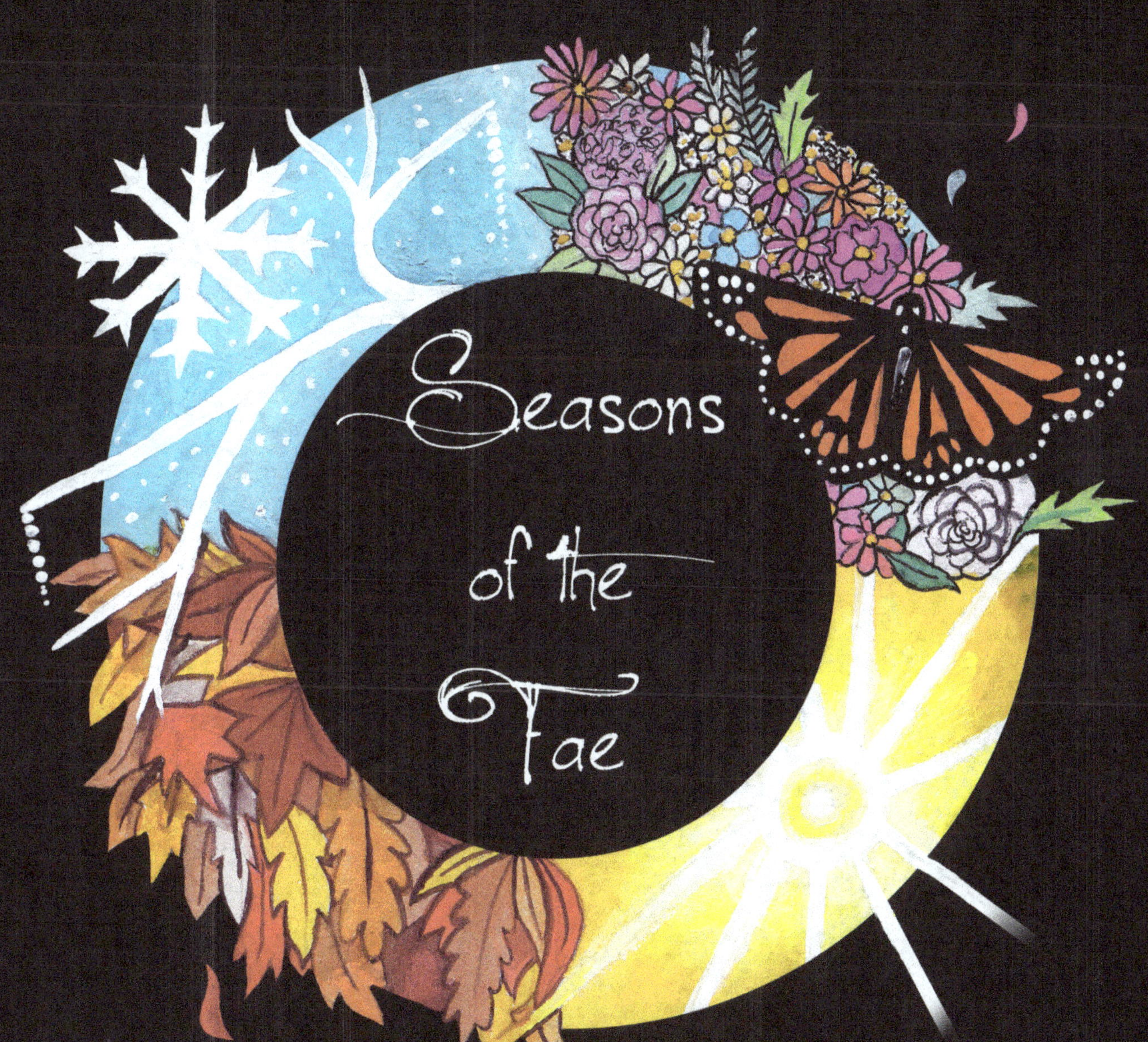
Seasons
of the
Fae

Summer

The days are long,
The sun is bright.
The Summer Lady,
Queen of light.

All is warmed,
With her golden glow.
The days are hot,
As life grows slow.

Soon the land,
Will begin to die.
The earth is parched,
The soil dry.

She wields the fire,
She rules the sun.
Her land is dying,
Until summer is done.

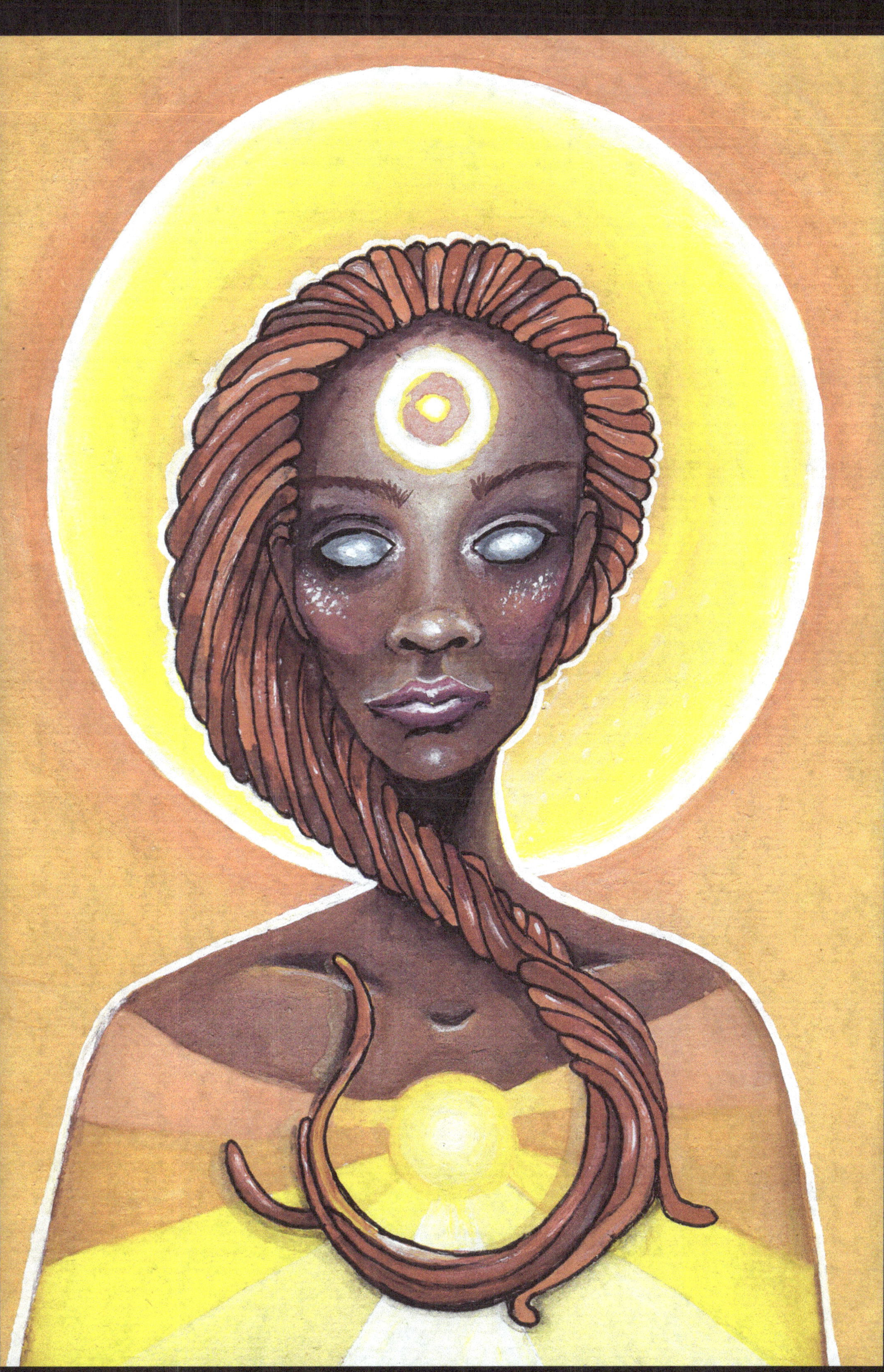

The Summer Lady

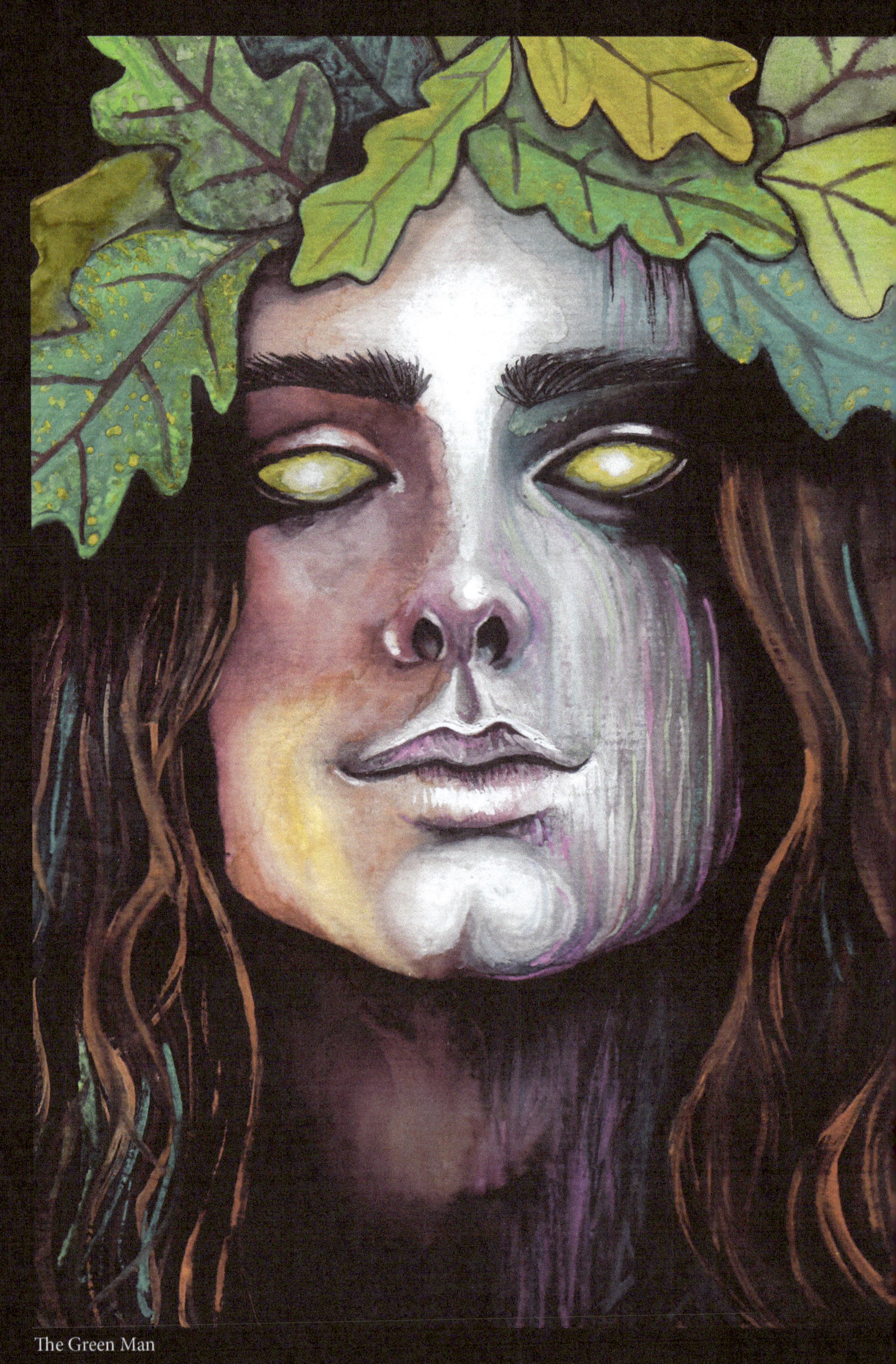

The Green Man

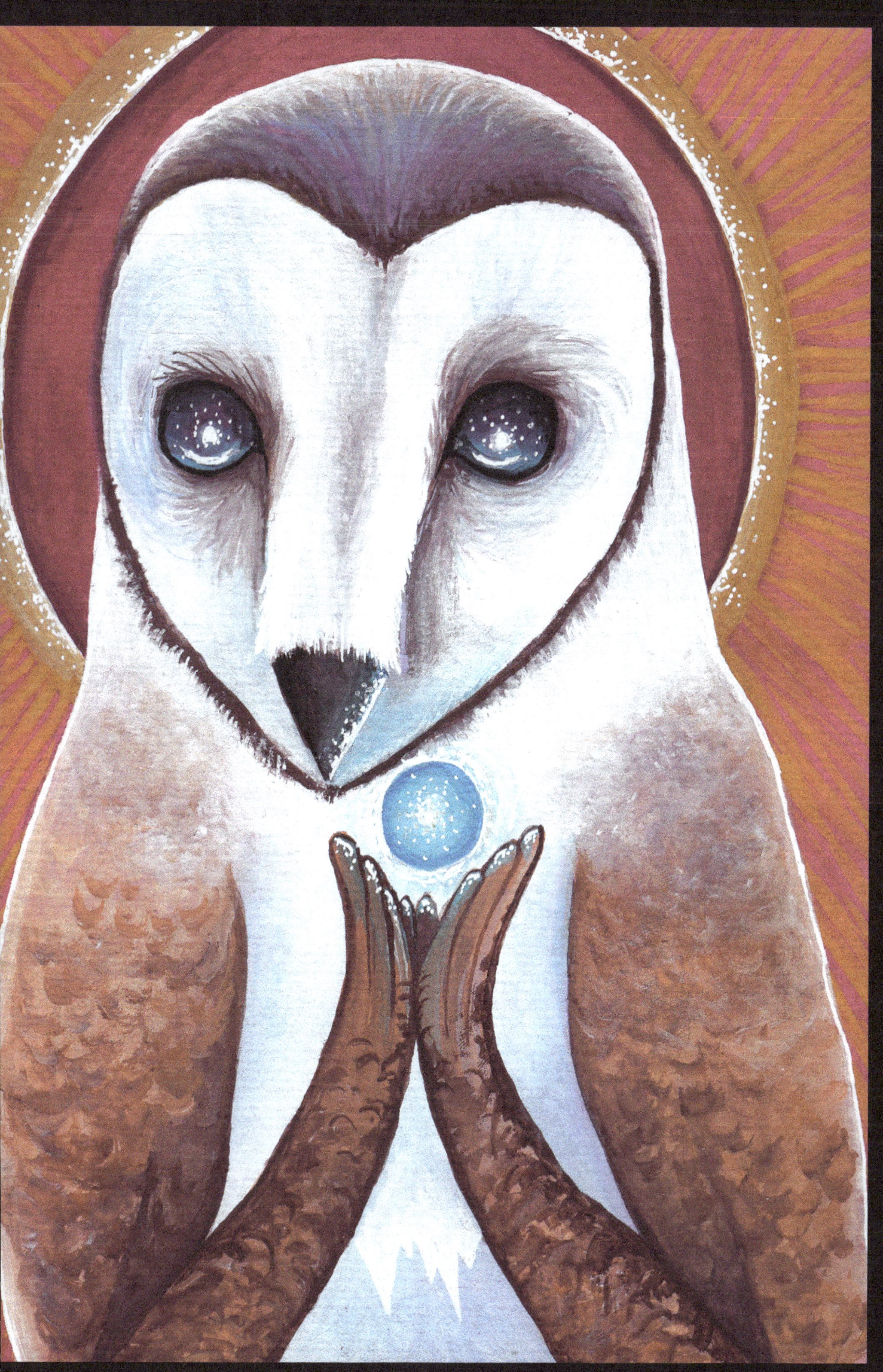

The Holy One

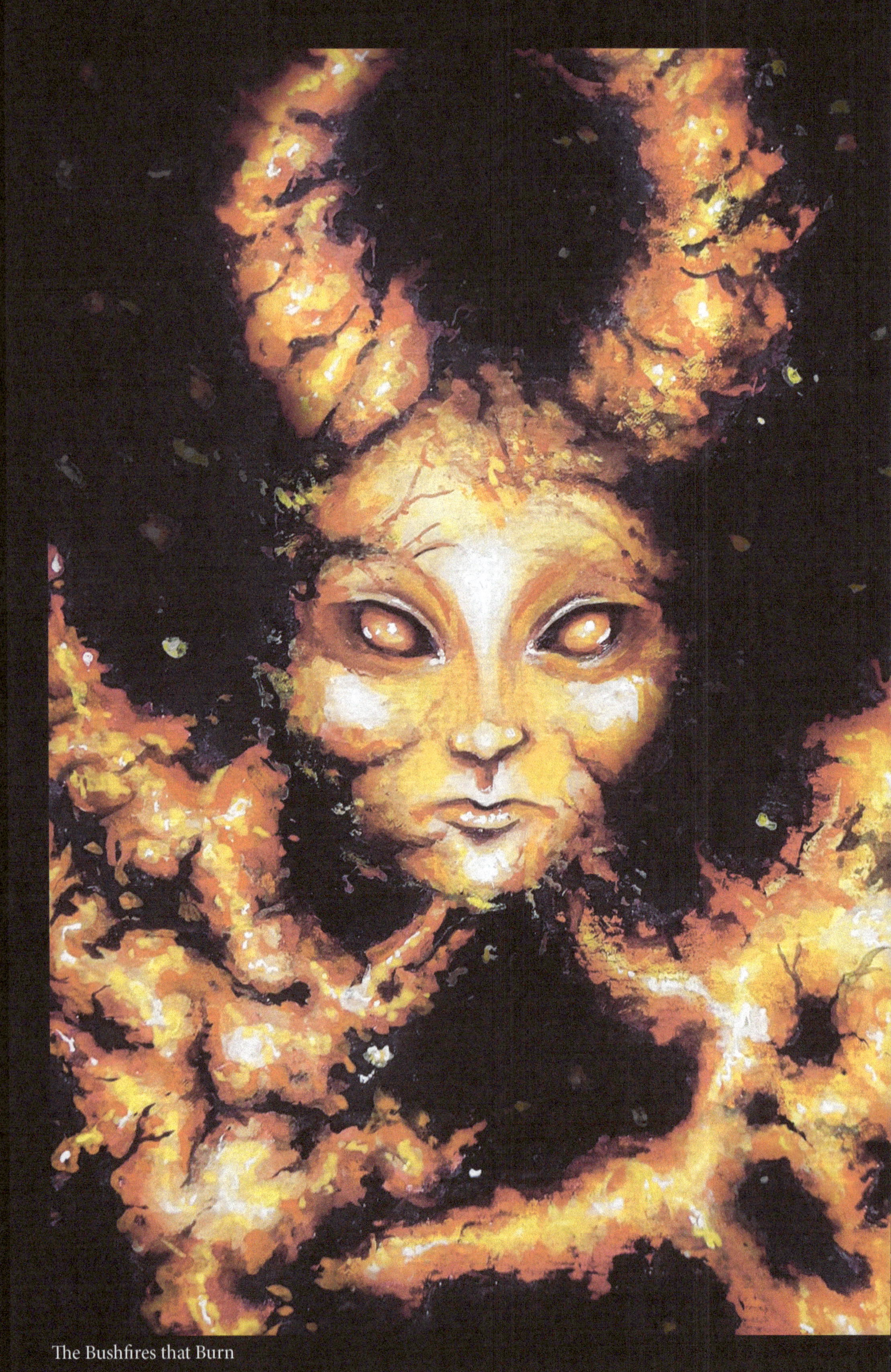

The Bushfires that Burn

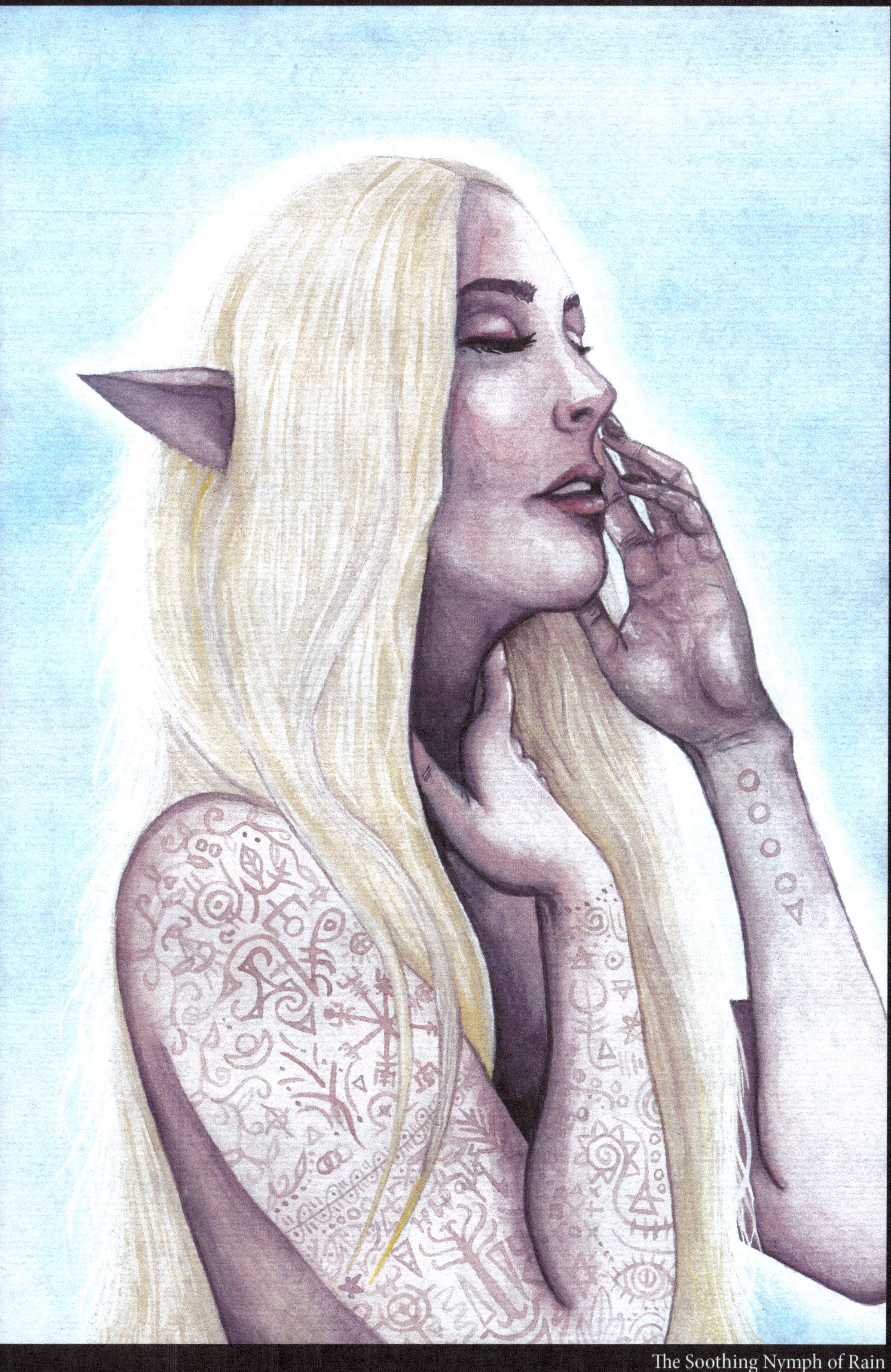

The Soothing Nymph of Rain

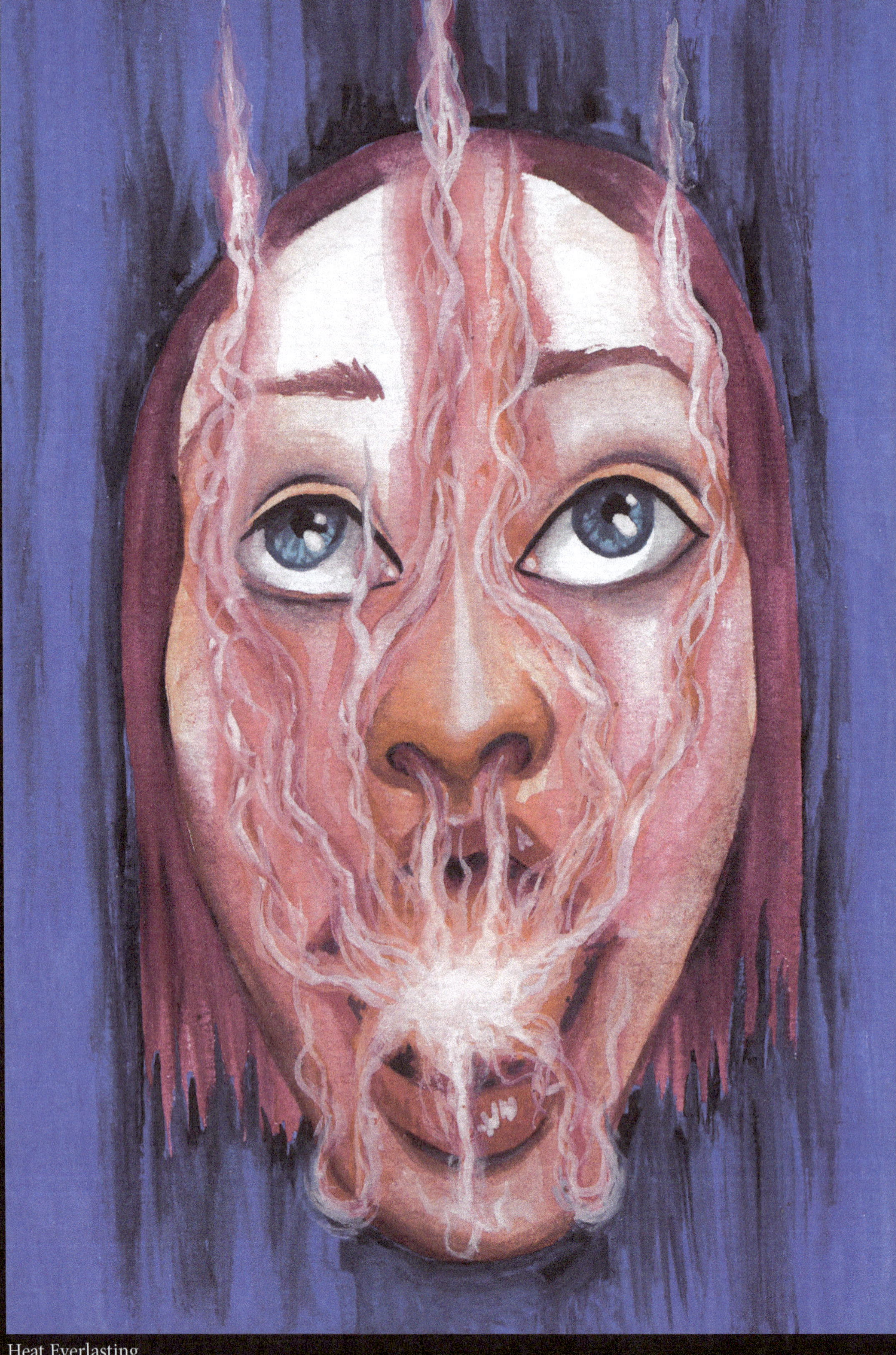

Heat Everlasting

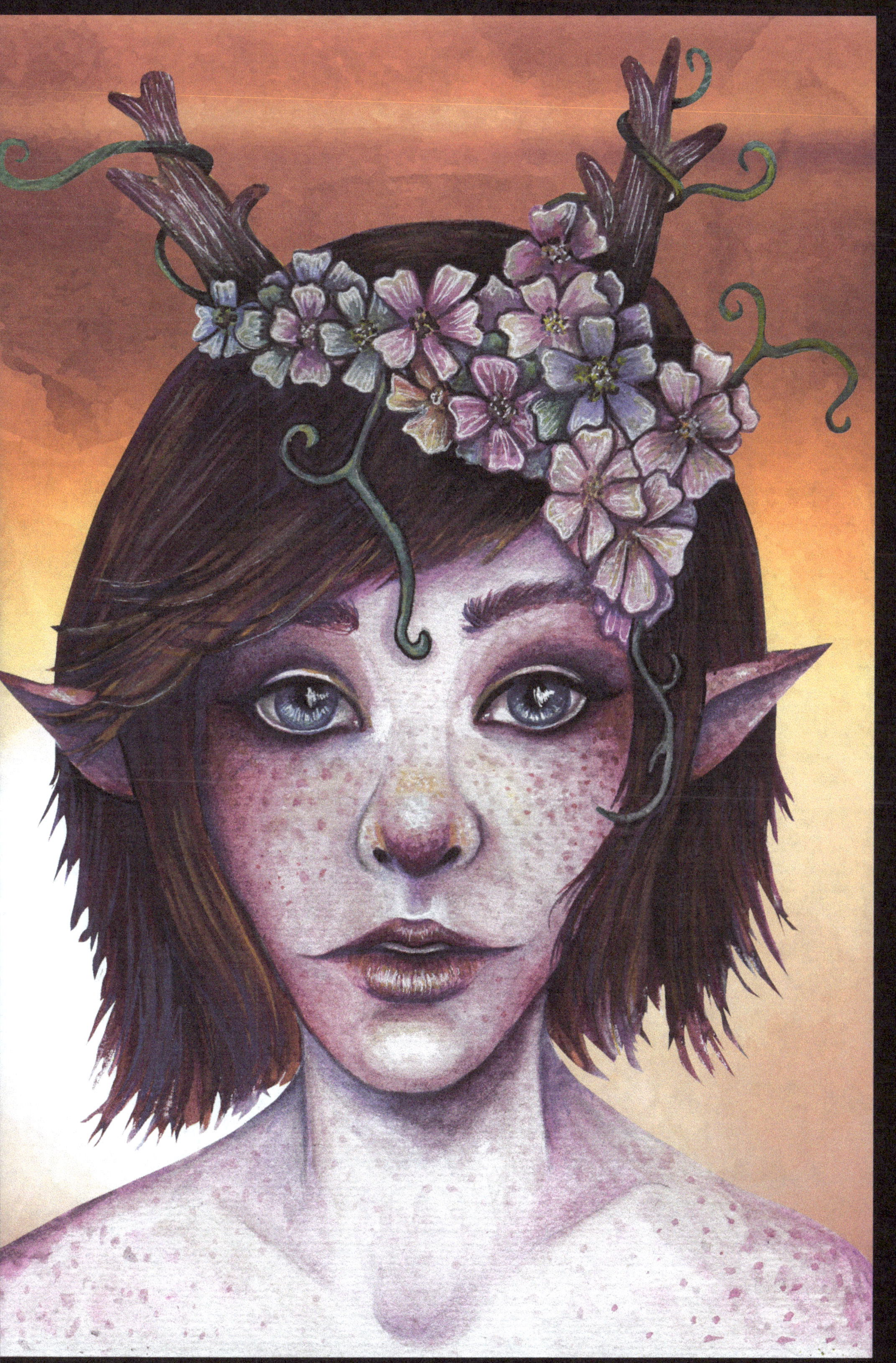

The Glow of Sunset

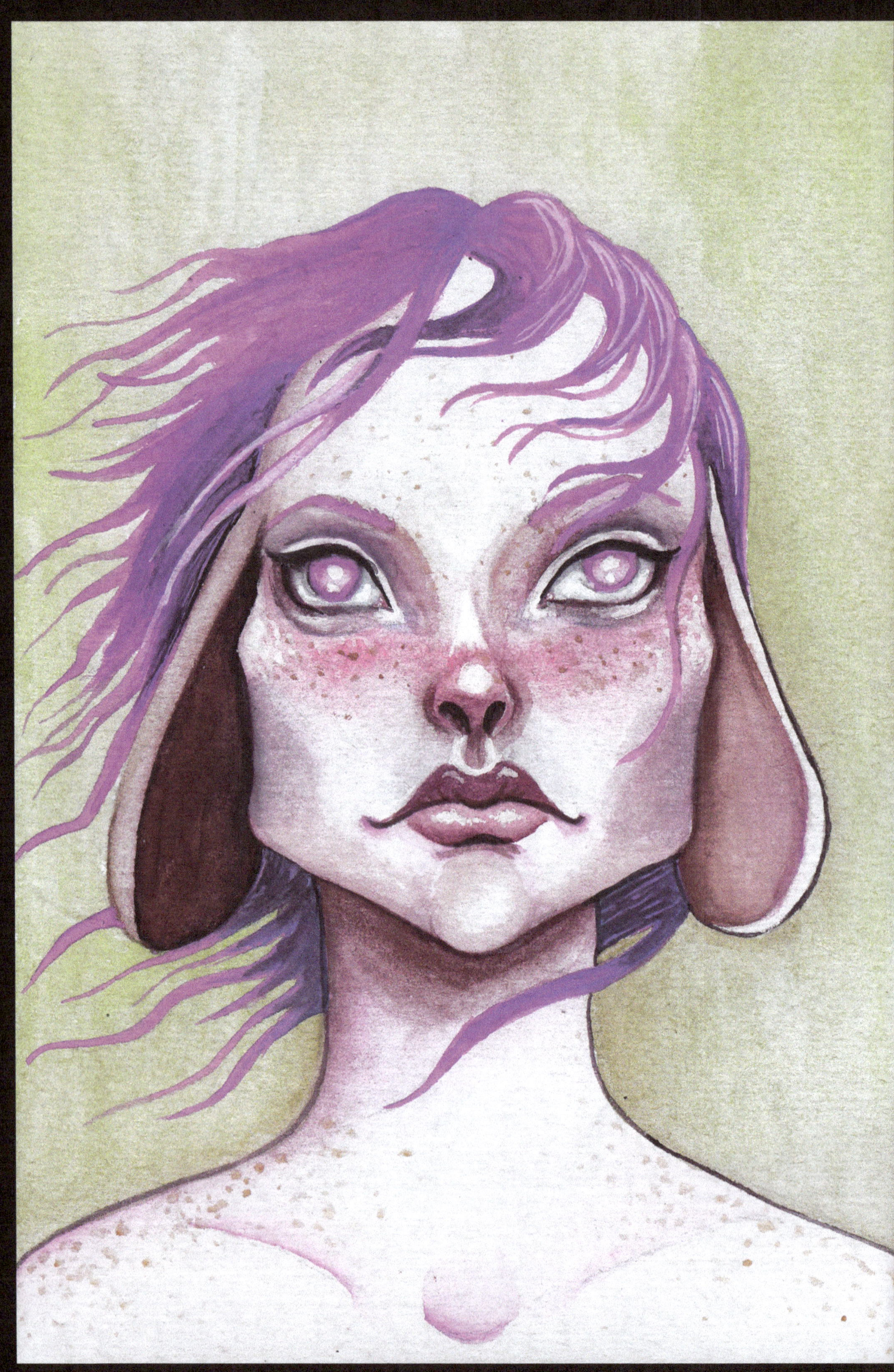

The Sunkissed Faun

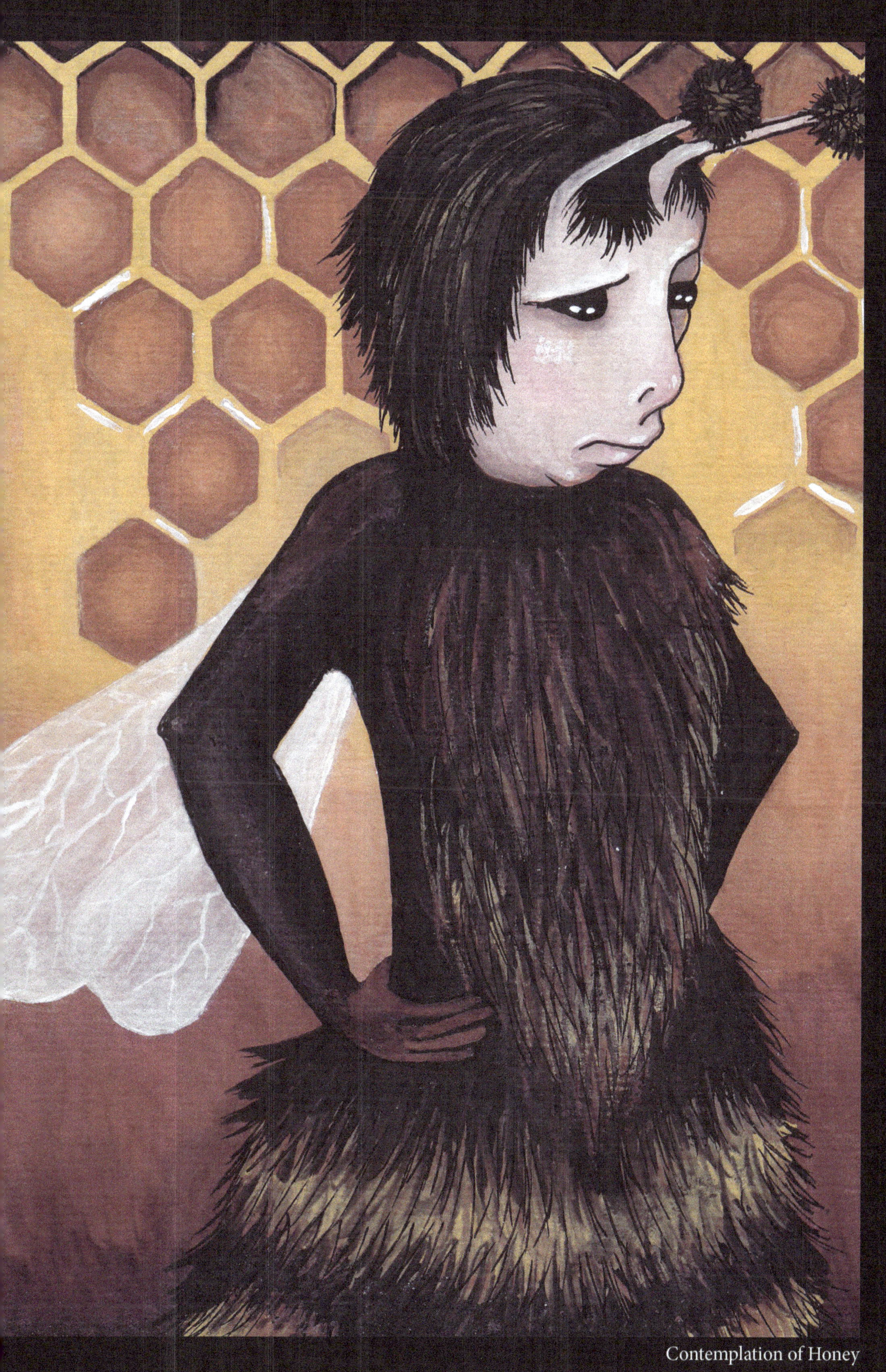

Contemplation of Honey

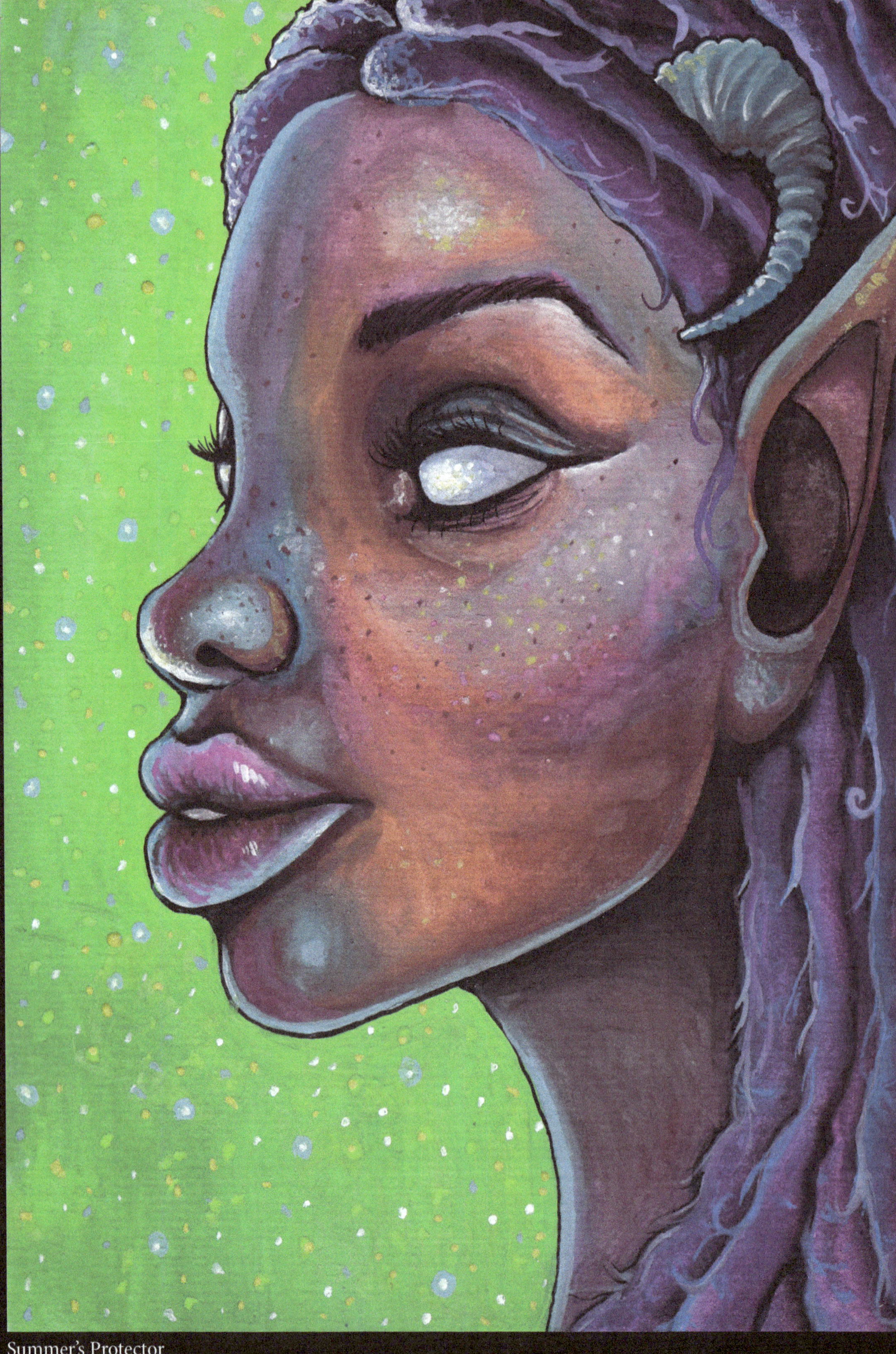

Summer's Protector

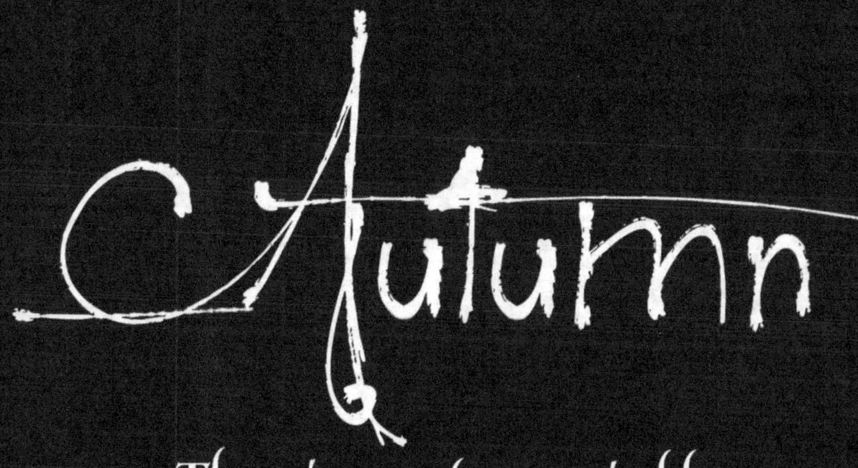

The green turns gold,
The green turns red.
The once bright life,
Is nearly dead.

Lady Autumn pulls,
Leaves to the ground.
A rust coloured carpet,
Of rustling sound.

The wind blows through,
The growing night.
The world readies to sleep,
In the death of the light.

The harvest has come,
Soon the feast will begin.
As they ready for winter,
As the veil grows thin.

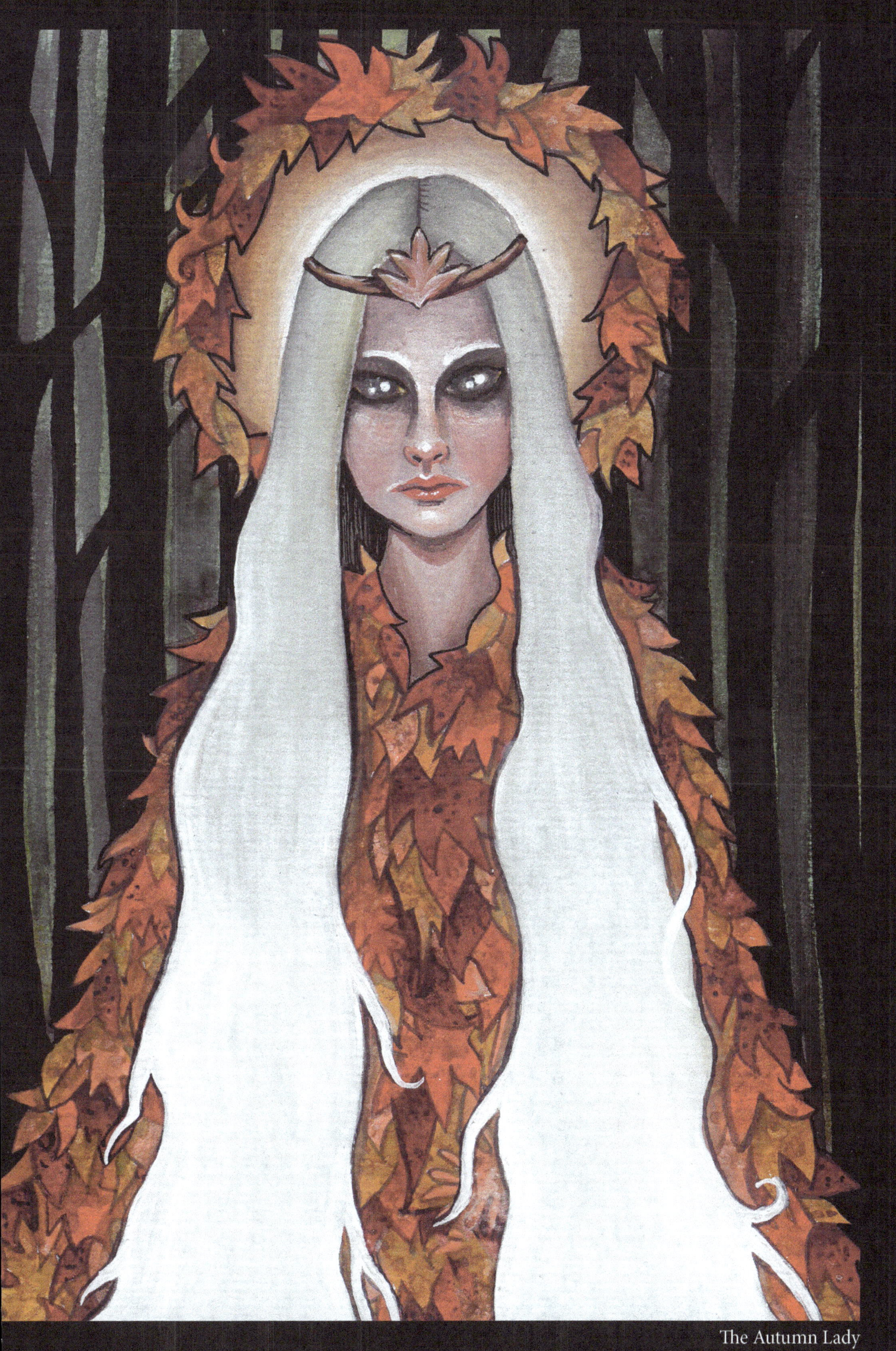

The Autumn Lady

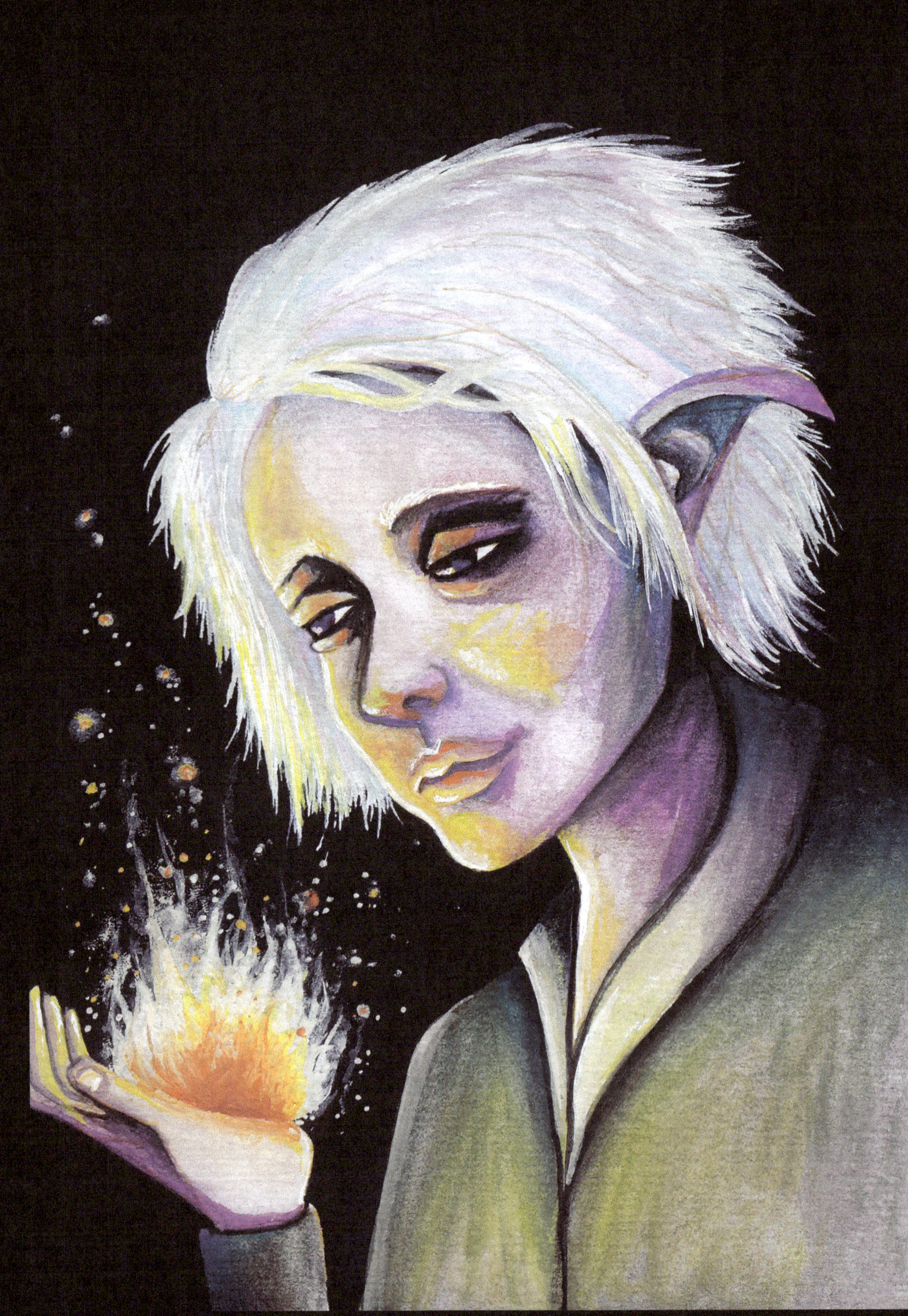

Bonfire Nymph

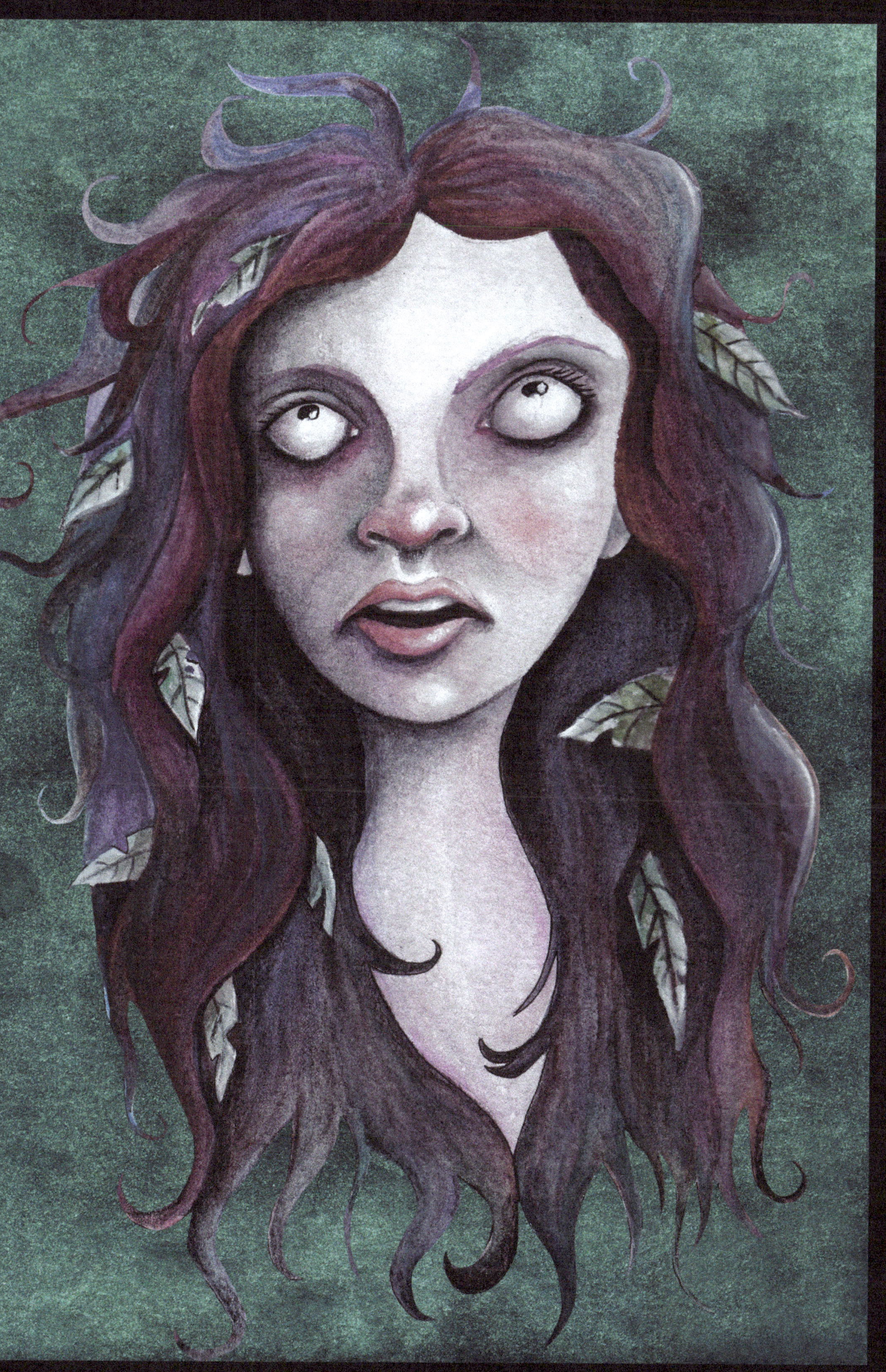

Leaves are Falling

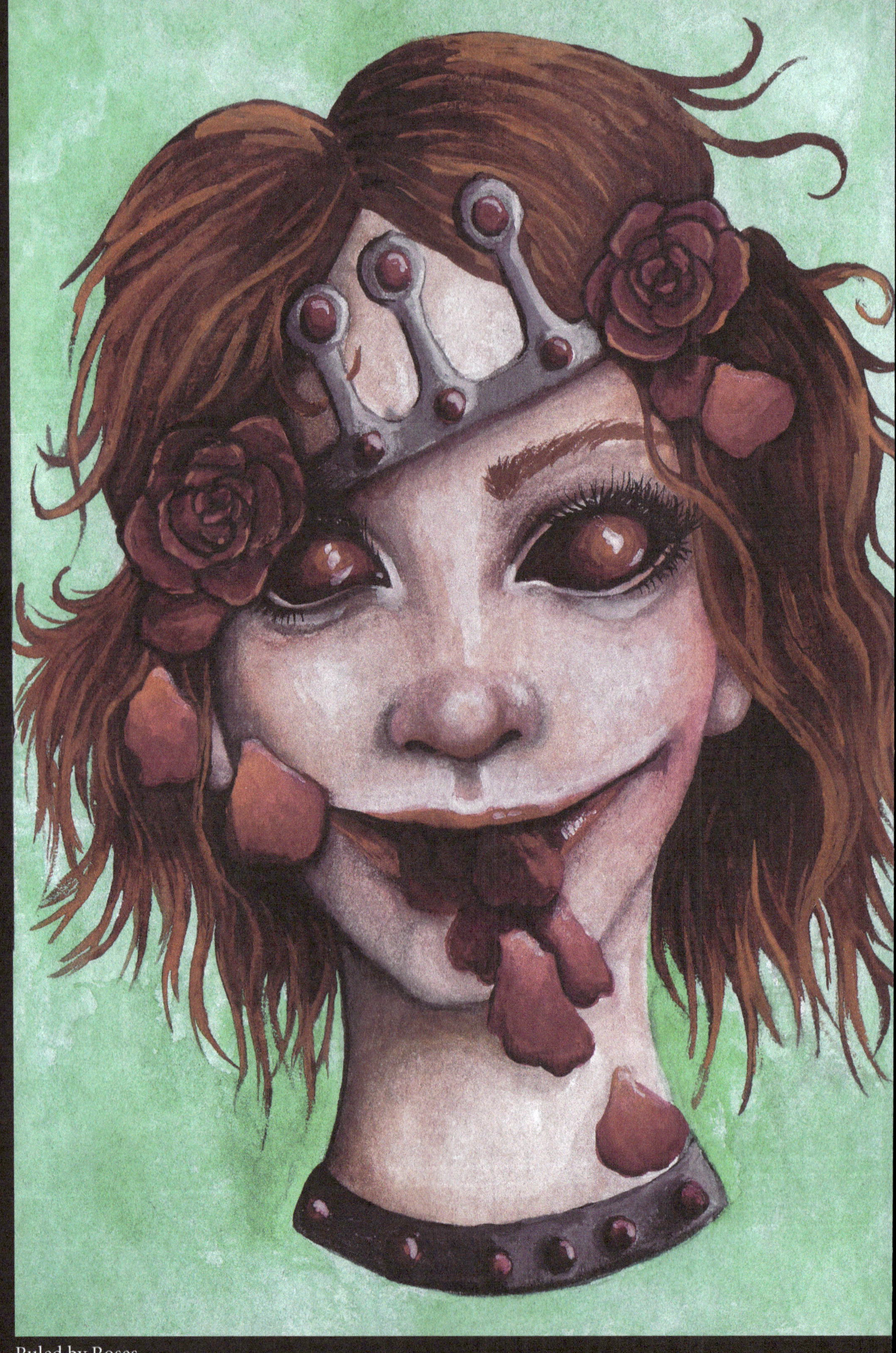

Ruled by Roses

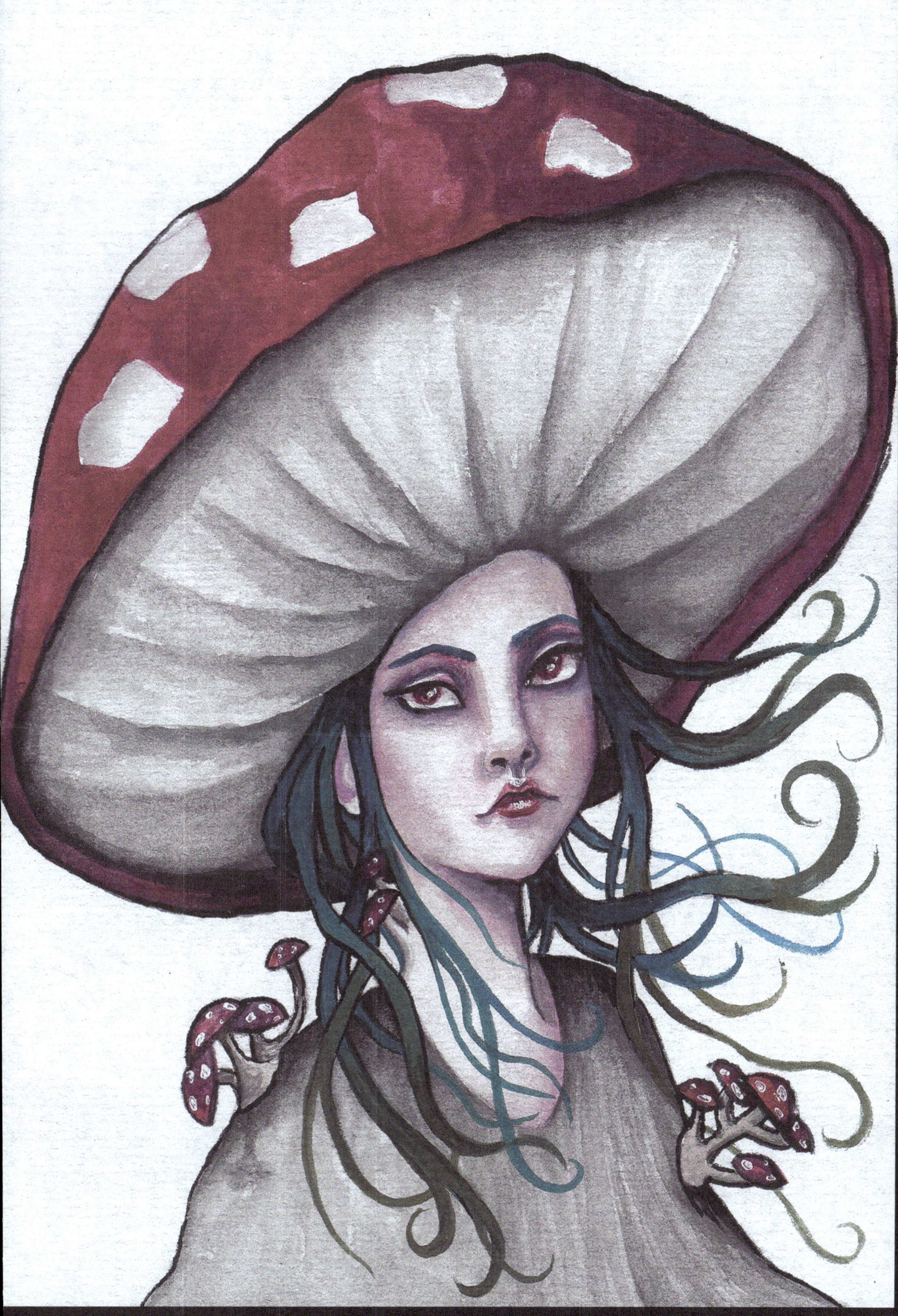

Mushrooms in the Wind

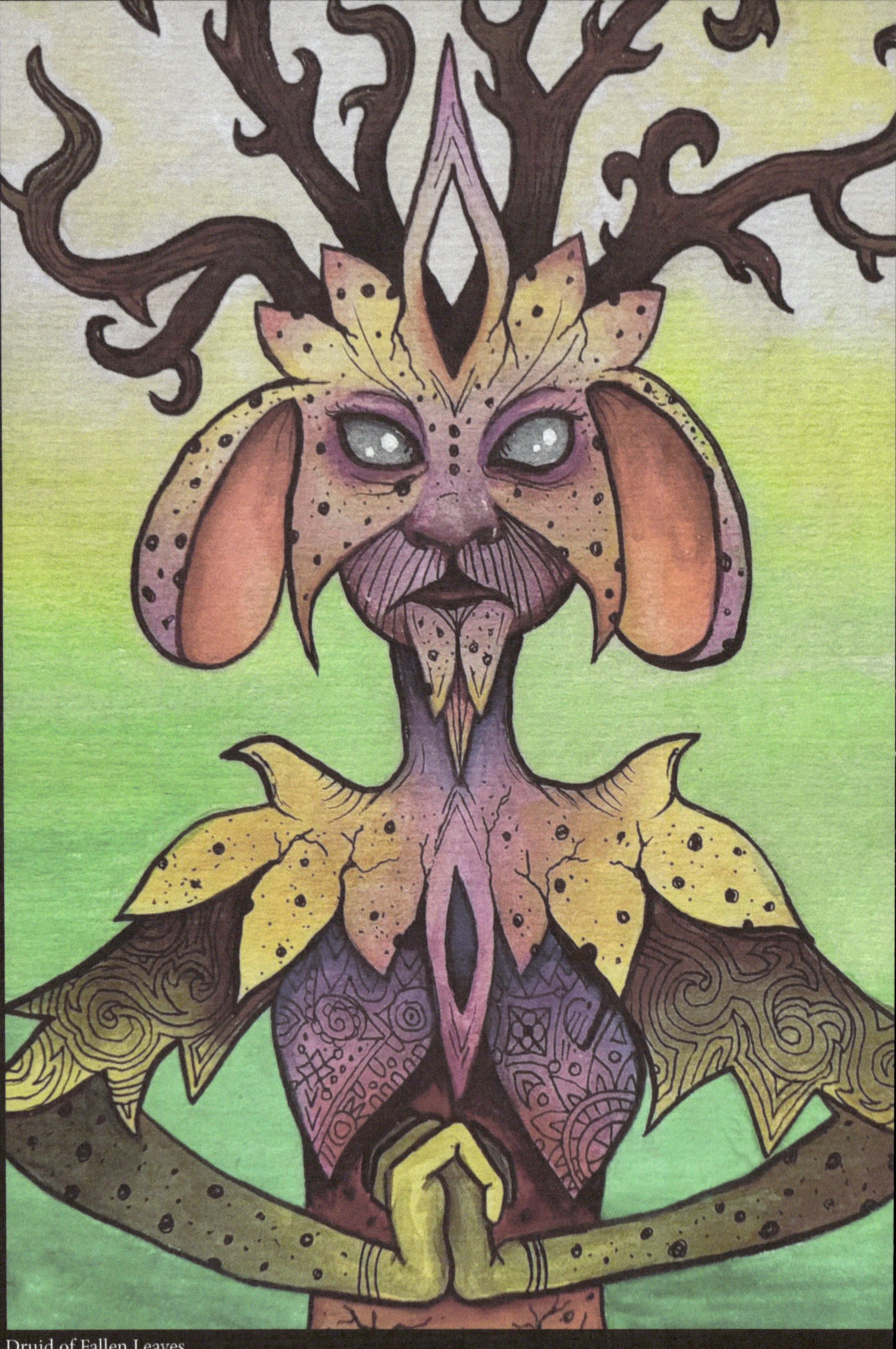

Druid of Fallen Leaves

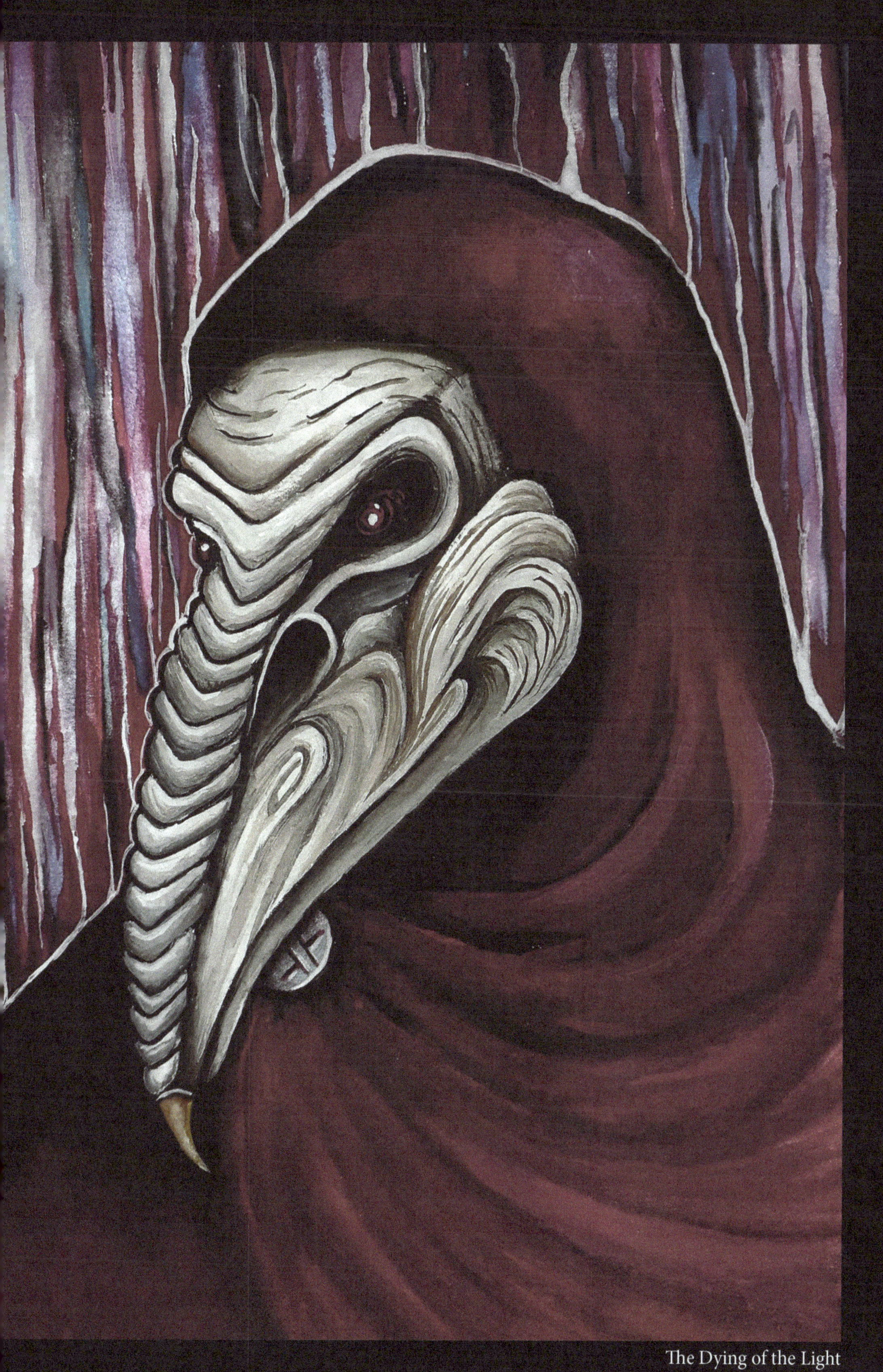

The Dying of the Light

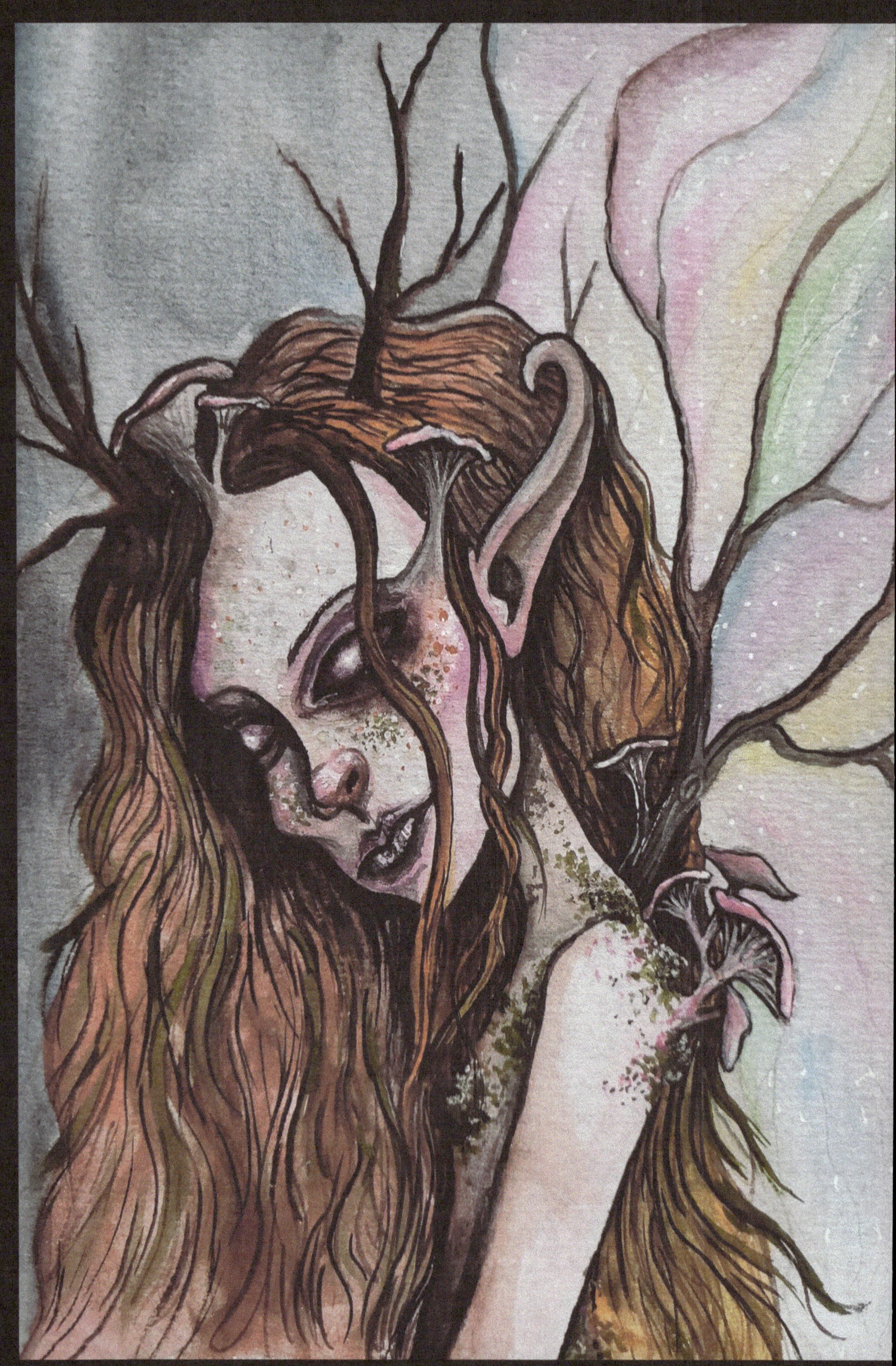

Life in Decay

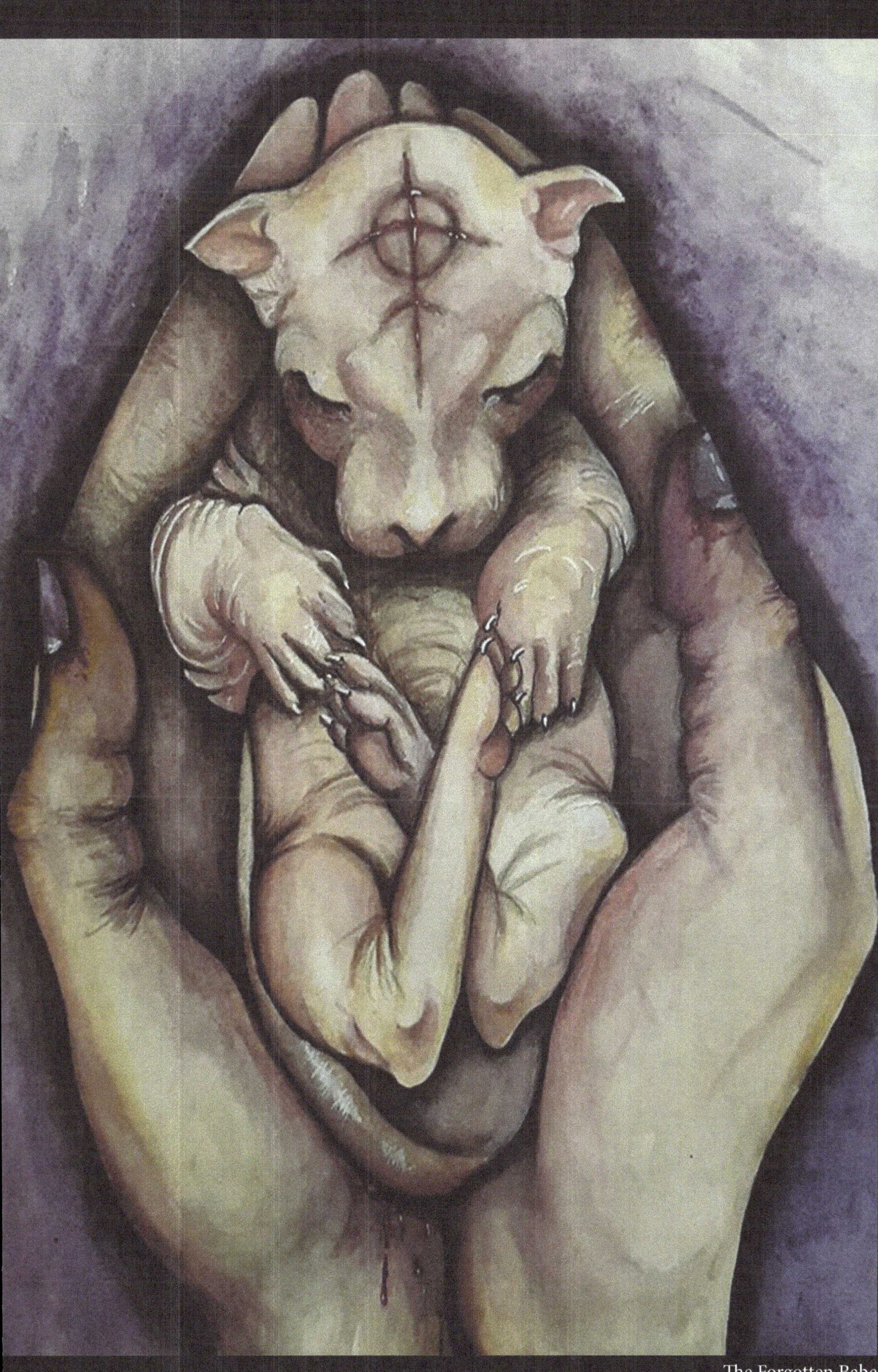

The Forgotten Babe

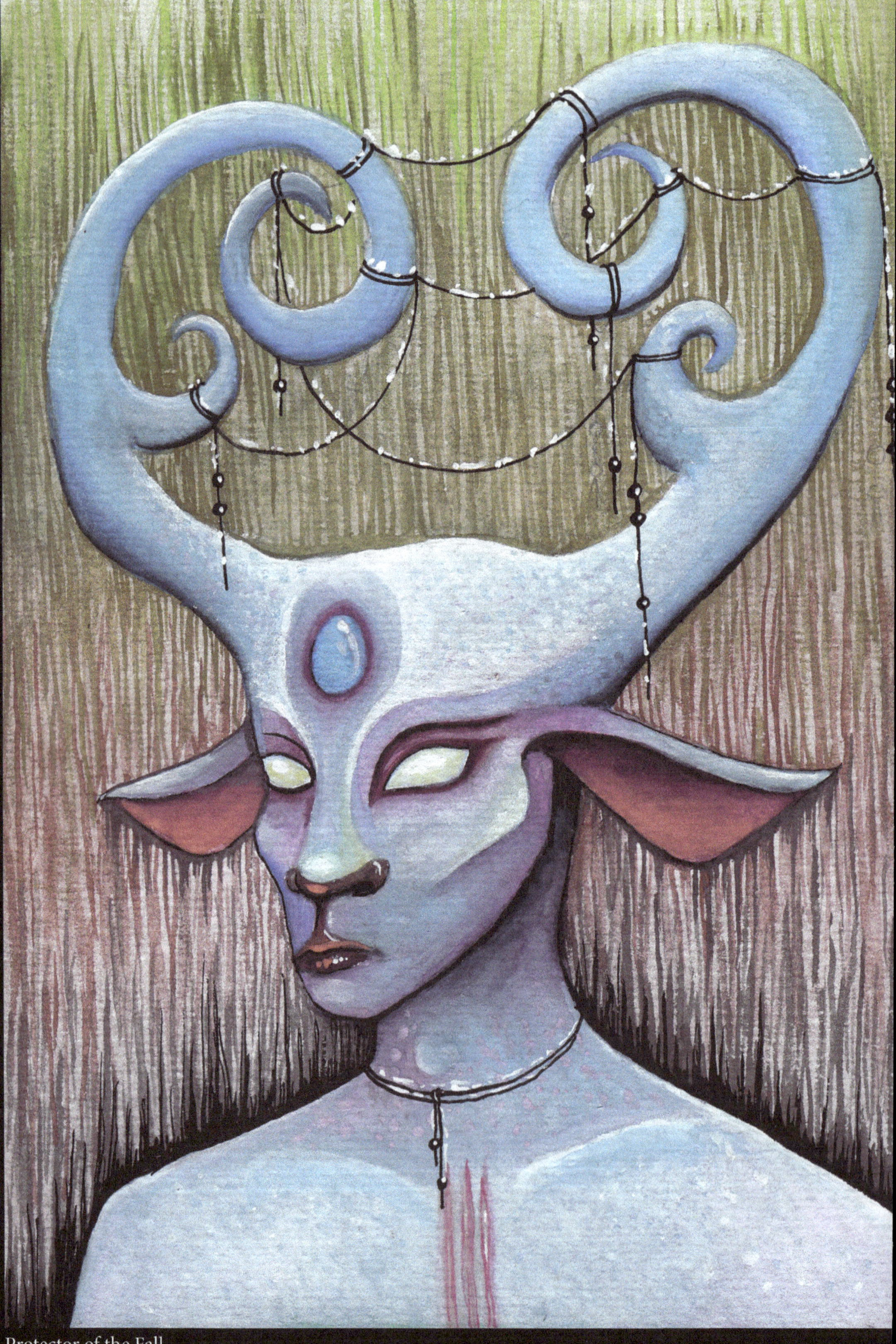

Protector of the Fall

Winter

The death has come,
And rebirth is nigh.
The Winter Lady,
Breathes a sigh.

Her touch is cold,
Her breath is sweet,
But soon the snow,
Melts at her feet.

She rules the dark,
Her forces strong.
Winter feasts,
When nights are long.

Soon she will slumber,
Soon she will weep,
As the winter winds,
Rock her to sleep.

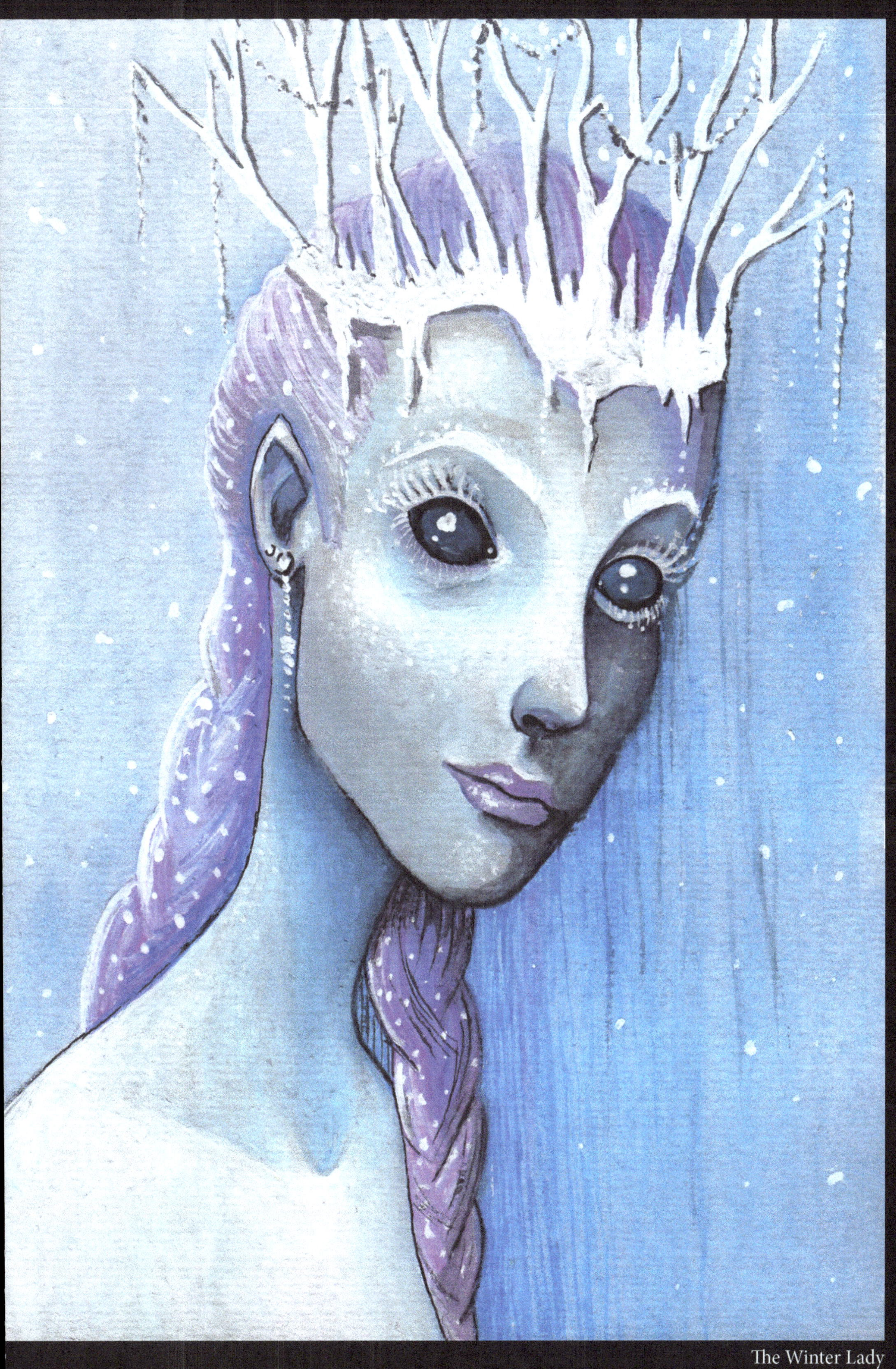

The Winter Lady

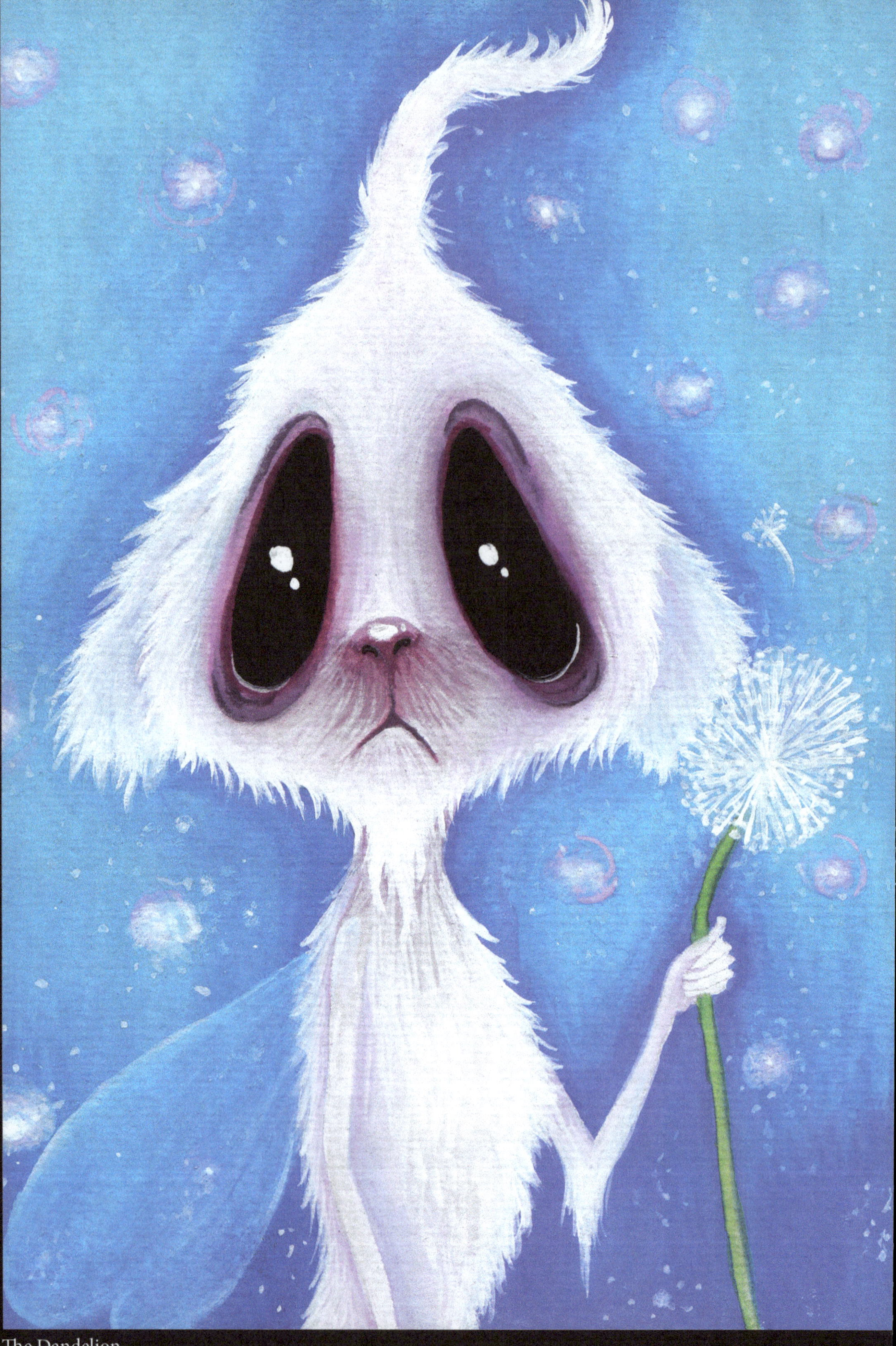

The Dandelion

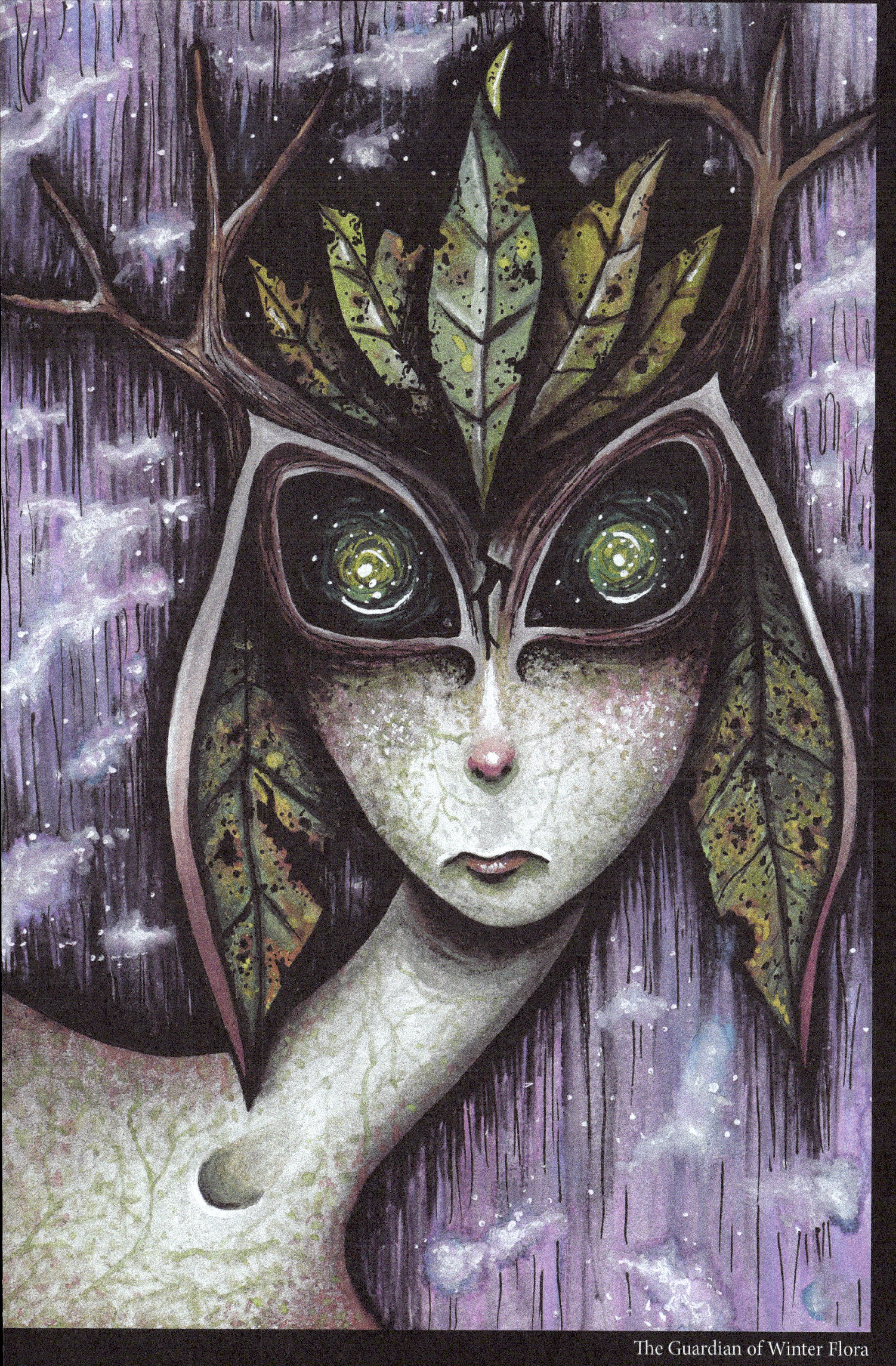

The Guardian of Winter Flora

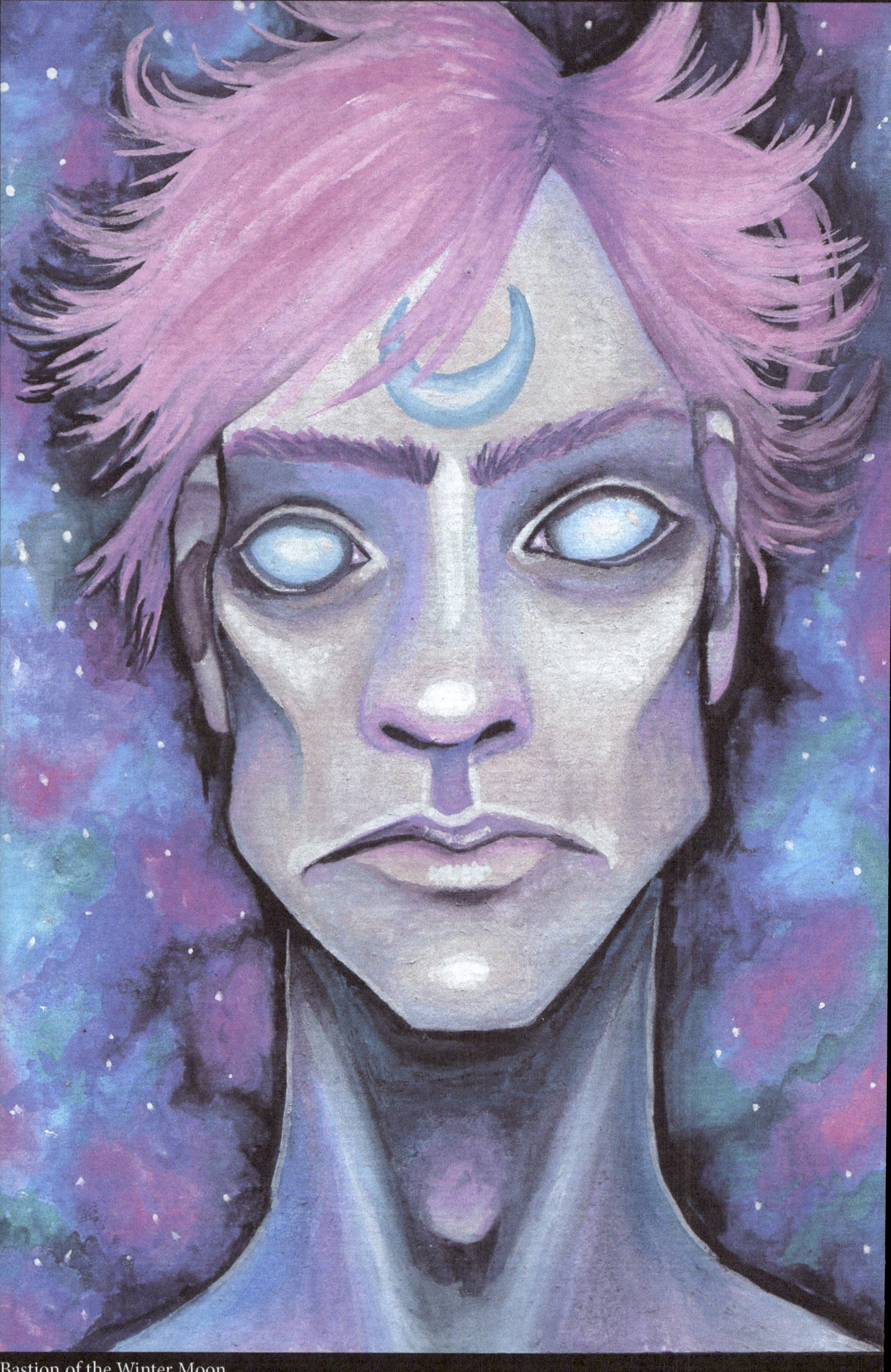

Bastion of the Winter Moon

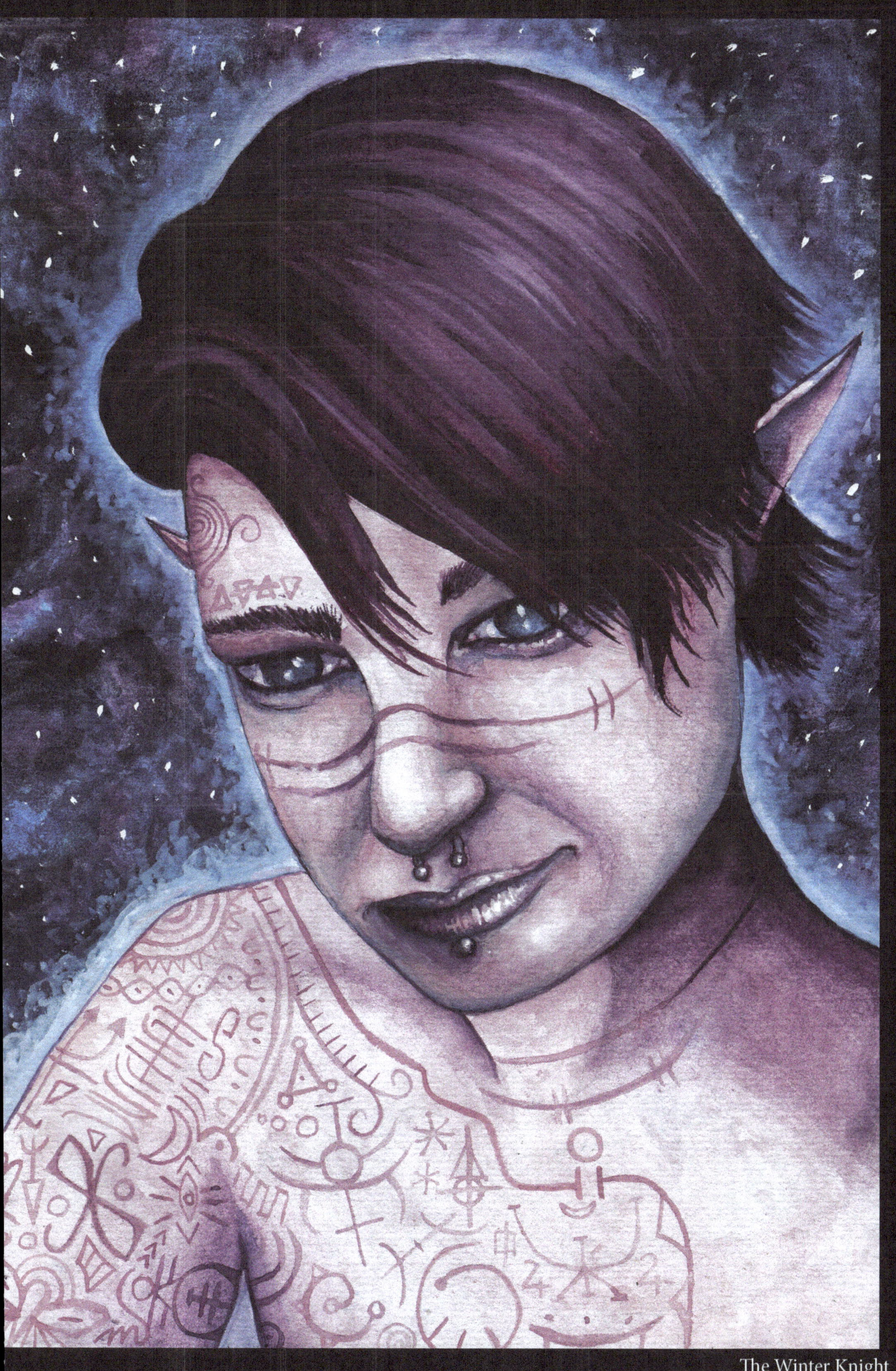

The Winter Knight

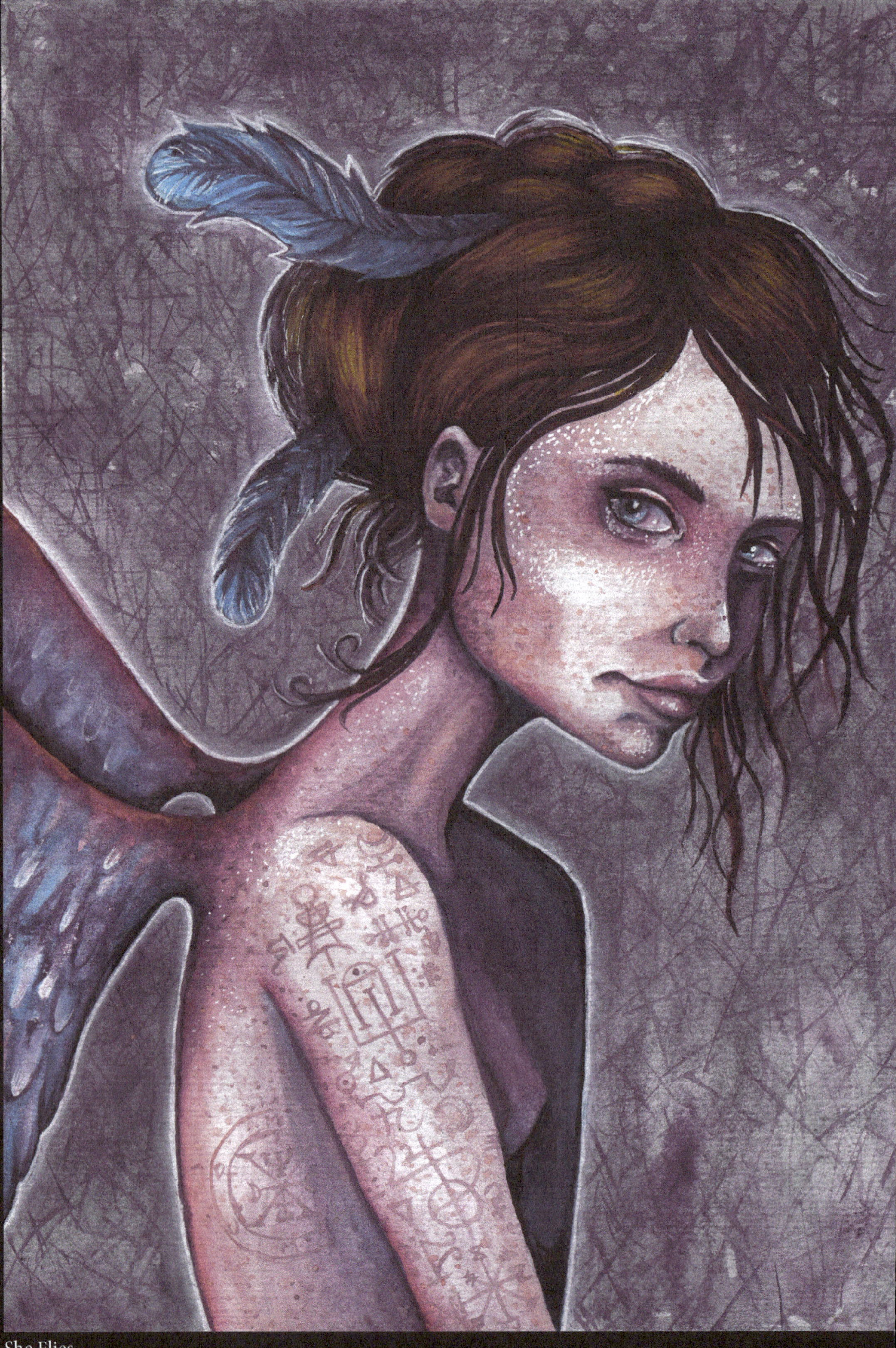

She Flies

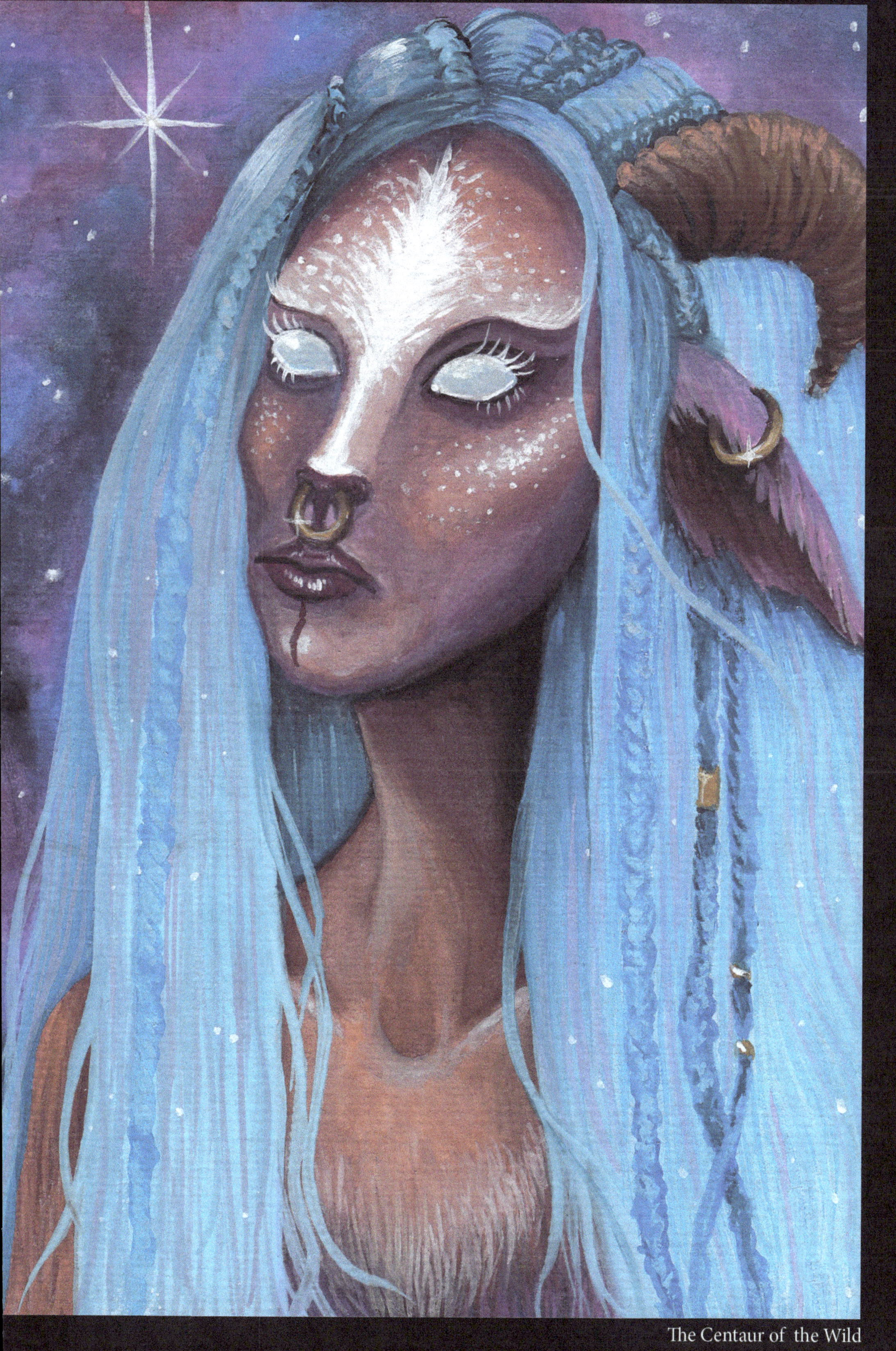

The Centaur of the Wild

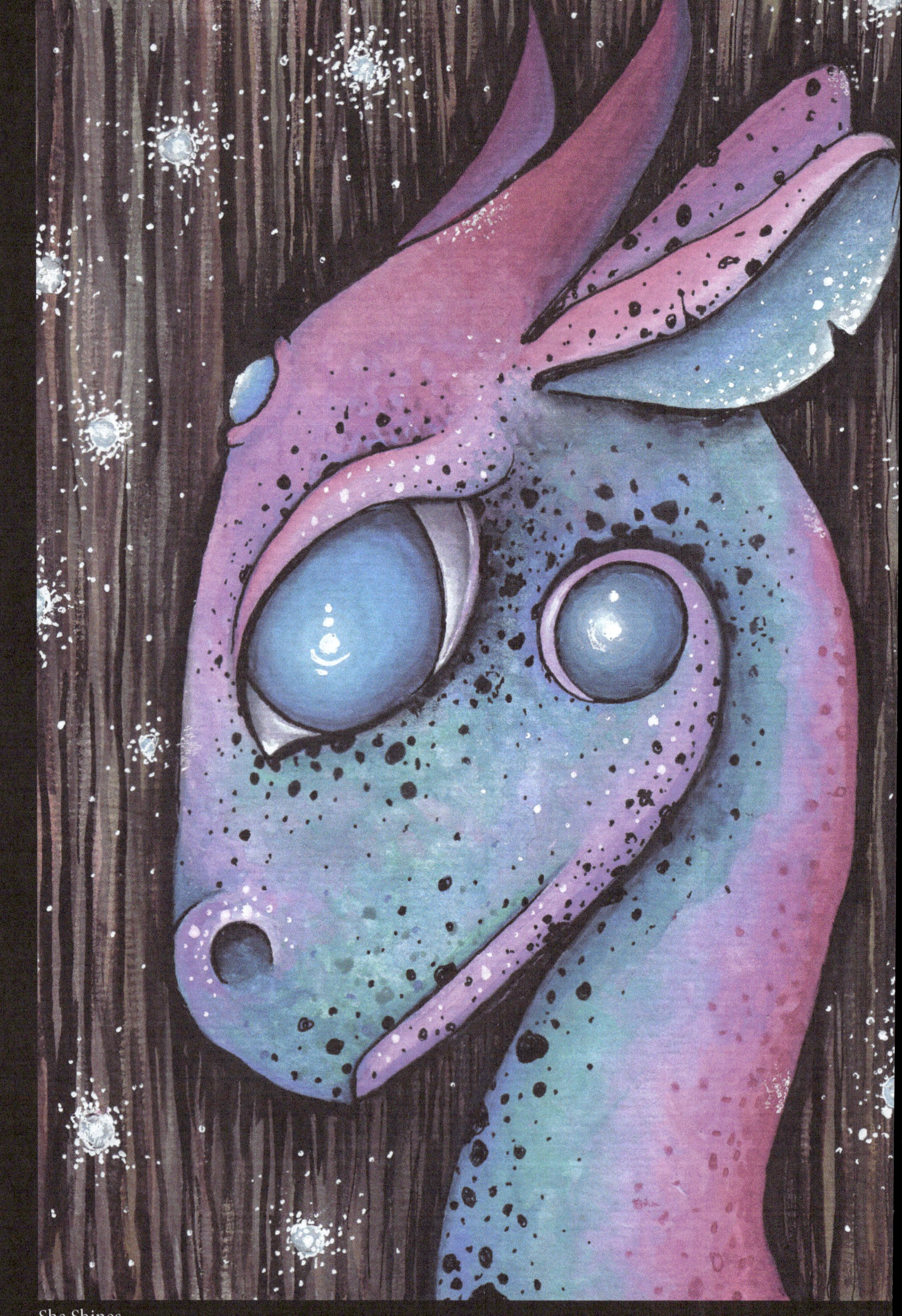

She Shines

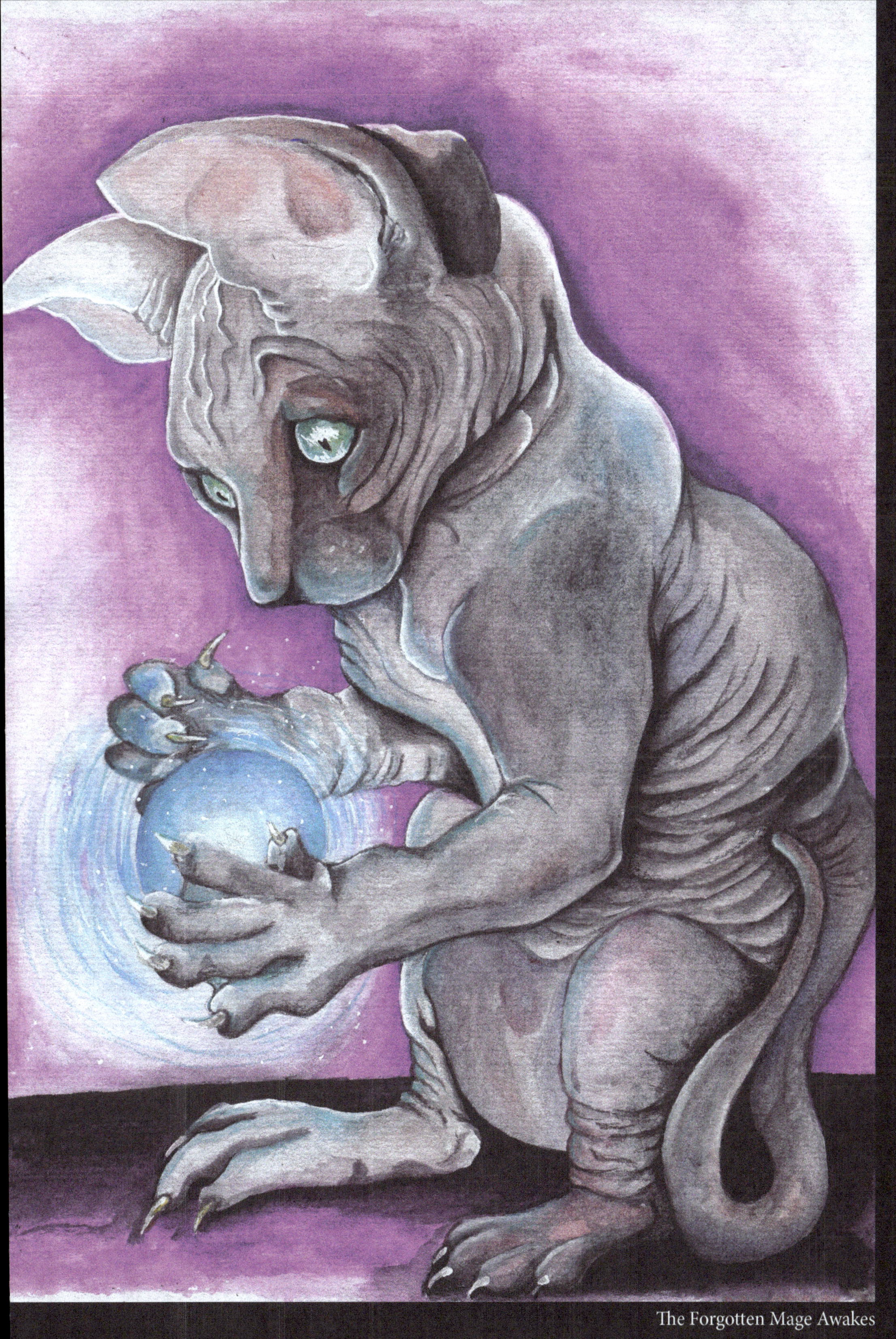

The Forgotten Mage Awakes

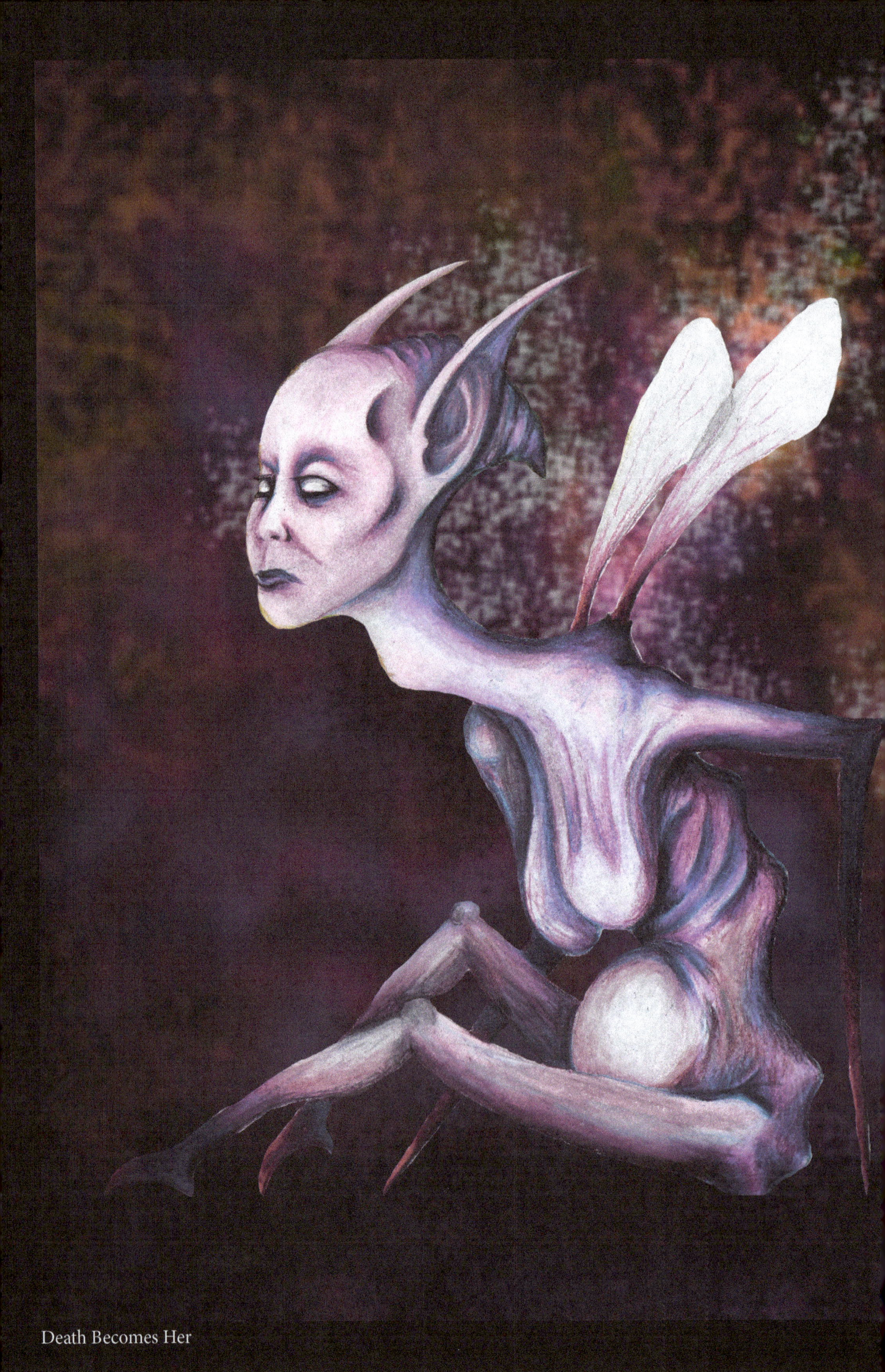

Death Becomes Her

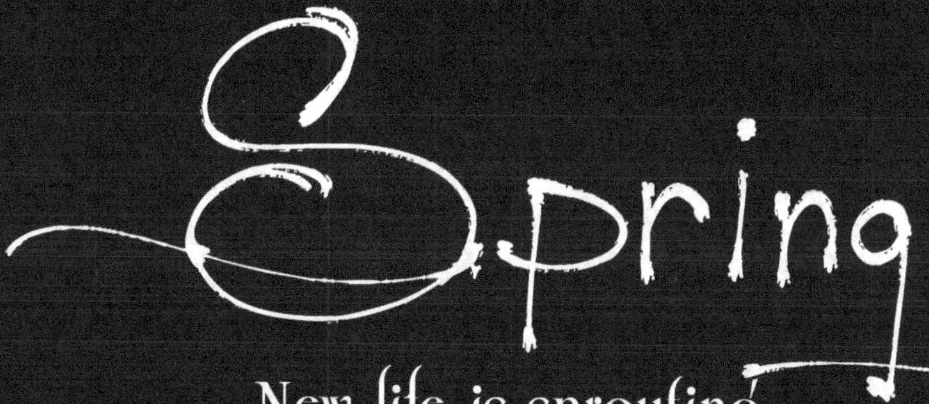

New life is sprouting,
Lady Spring has arrived.
Nature is singing,
Another winter survived.

Her spirit a flutter,
She blossoms and blooms.
A flurry of colour,
From petals to plumes.

Her creatures emerge,
As warmth fills their bones.
The air is all humming,
With musical tones.

The days grow longer,
The colours grow bright,
The Spring Lady's song,
Such a wonderful sight.

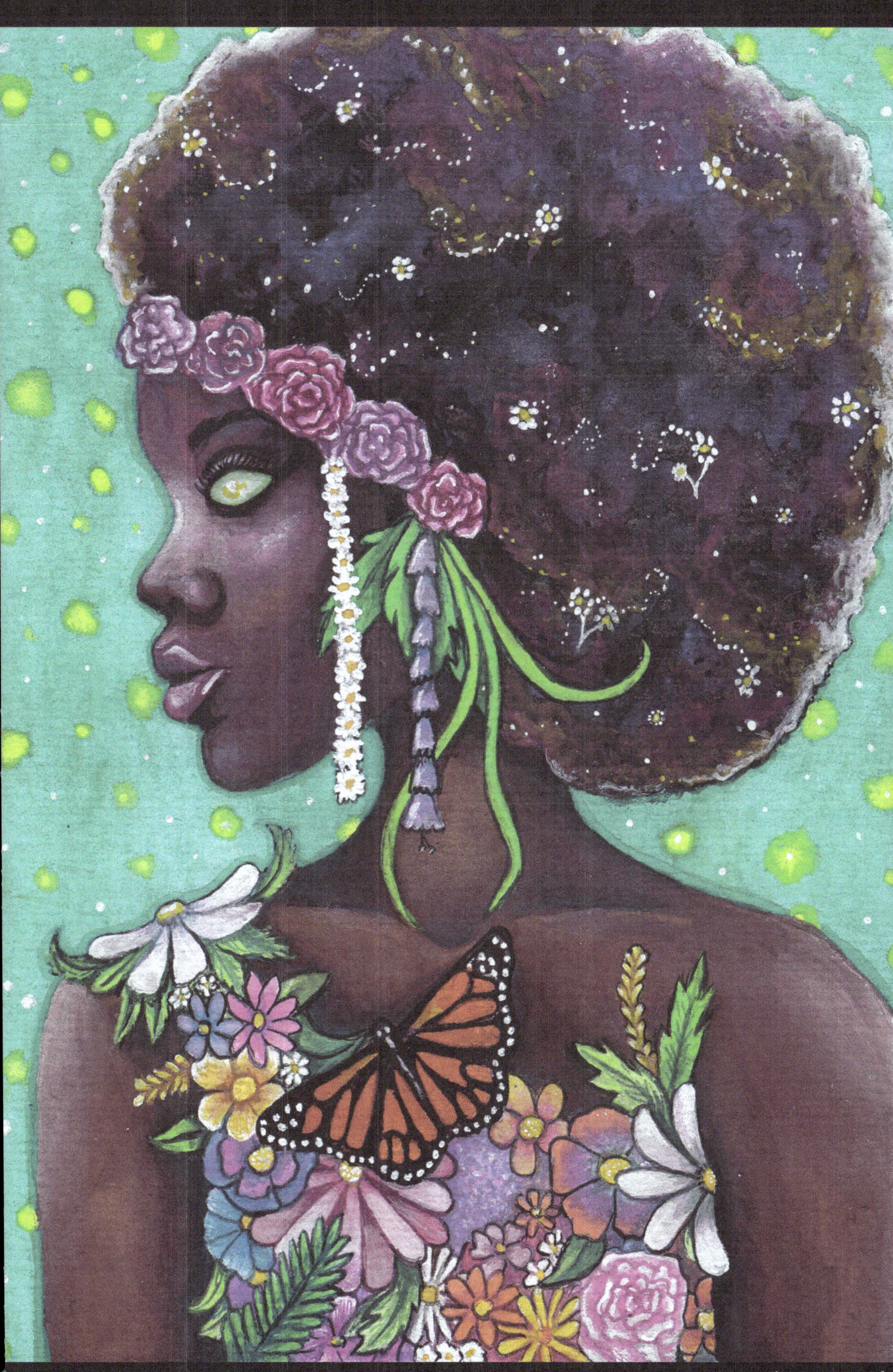

The Spring Lady

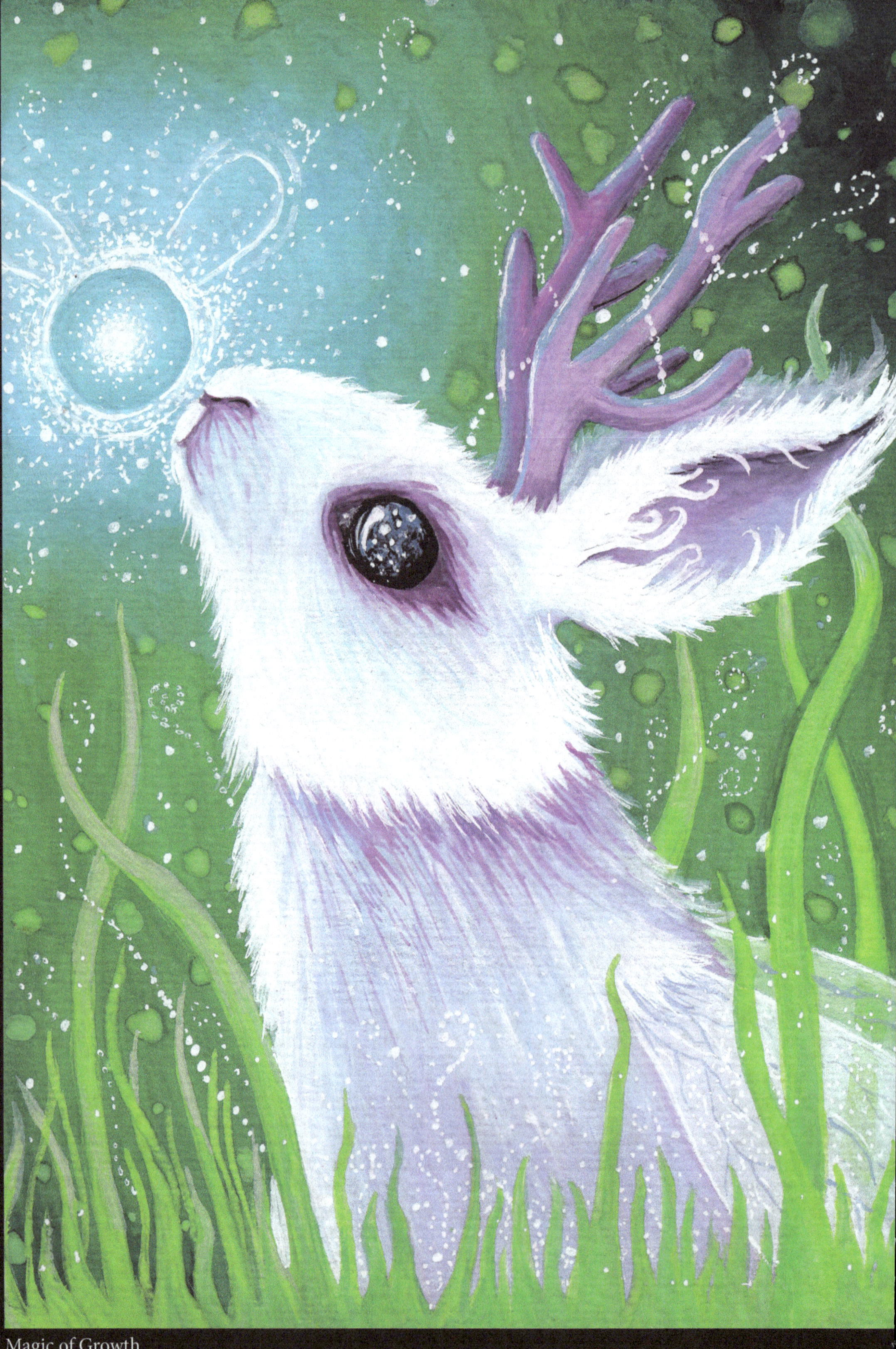
Magic of Growth

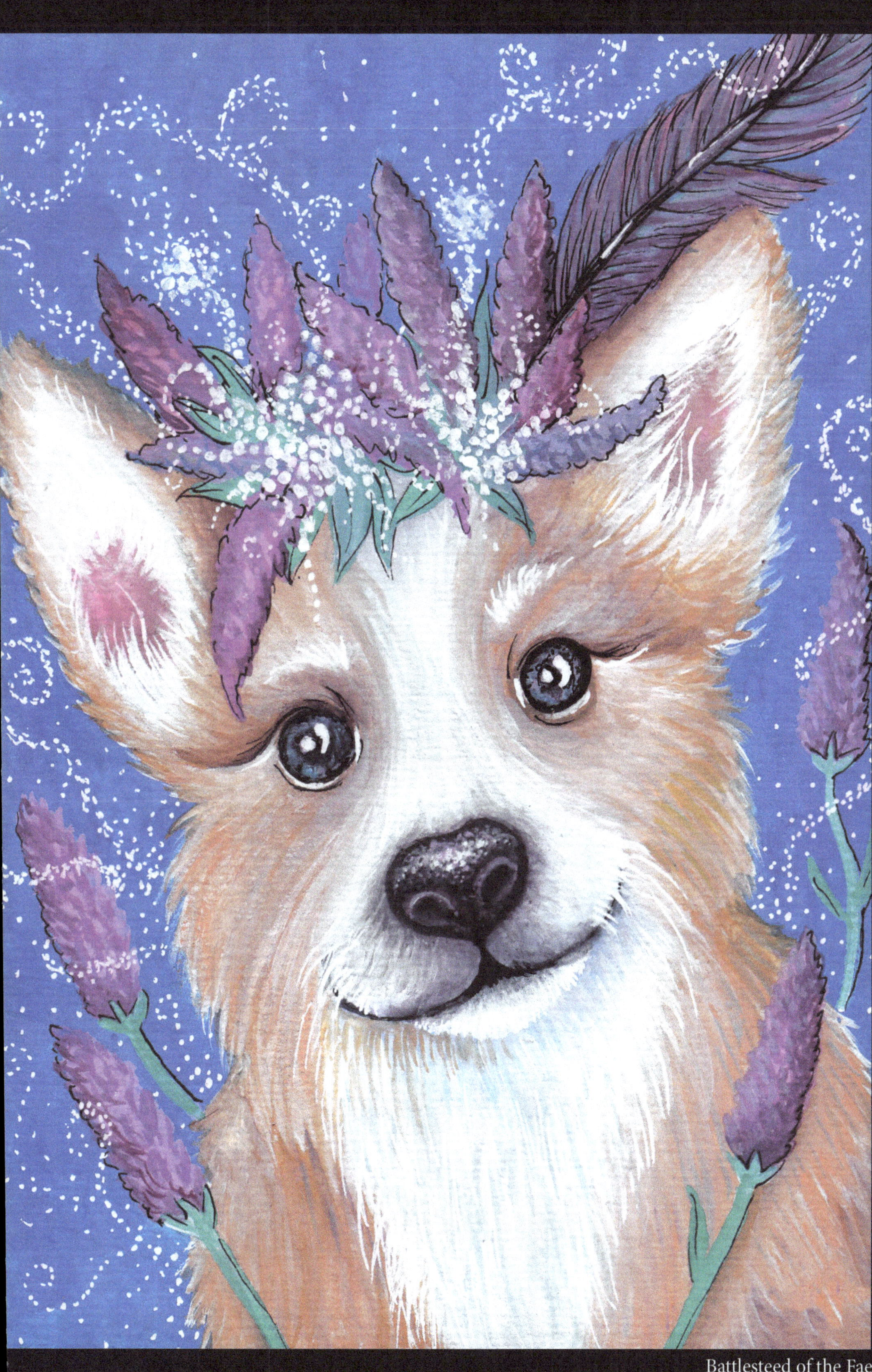

Battlesteed of the Fae

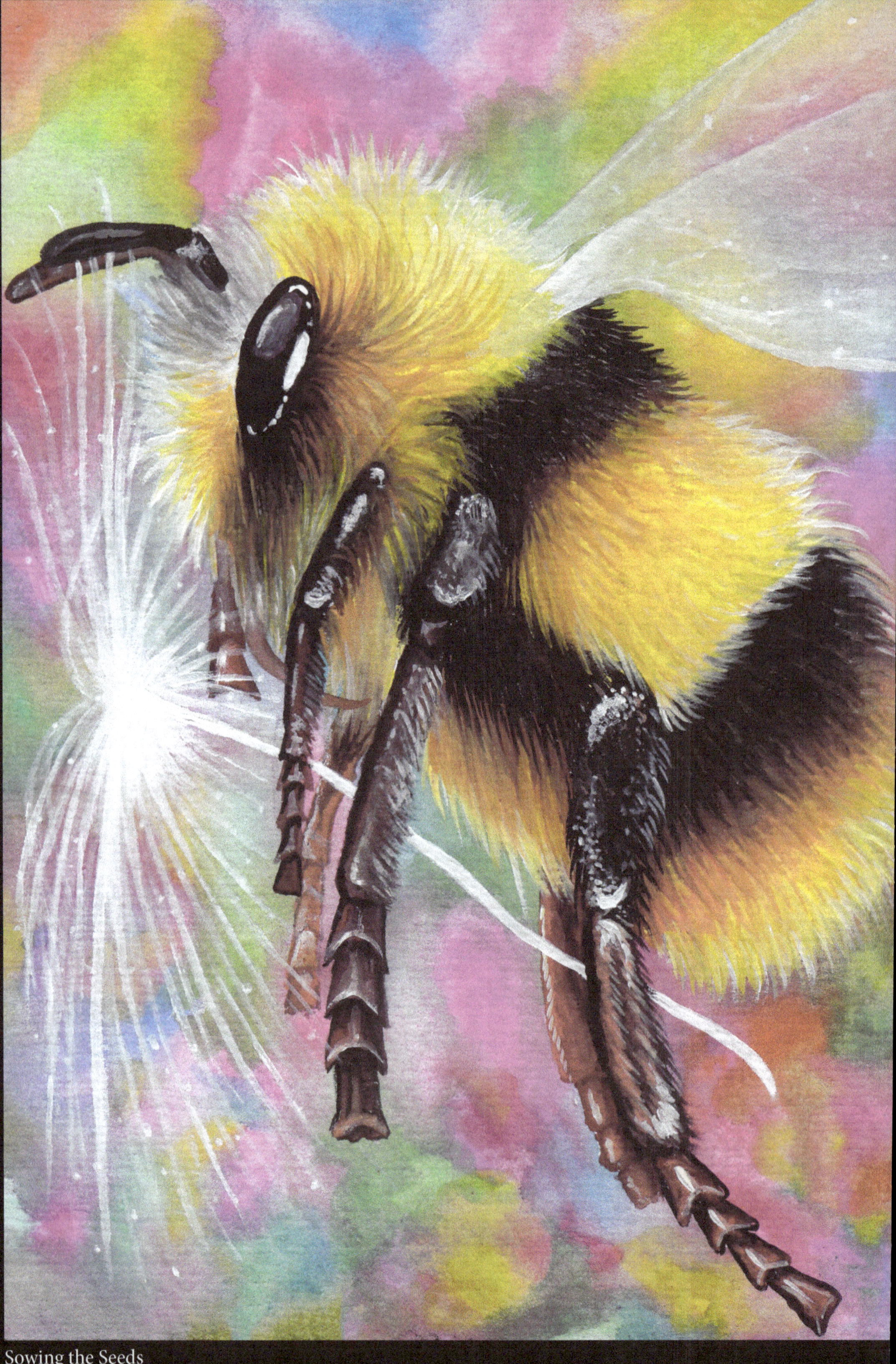

Sowing the Seeds

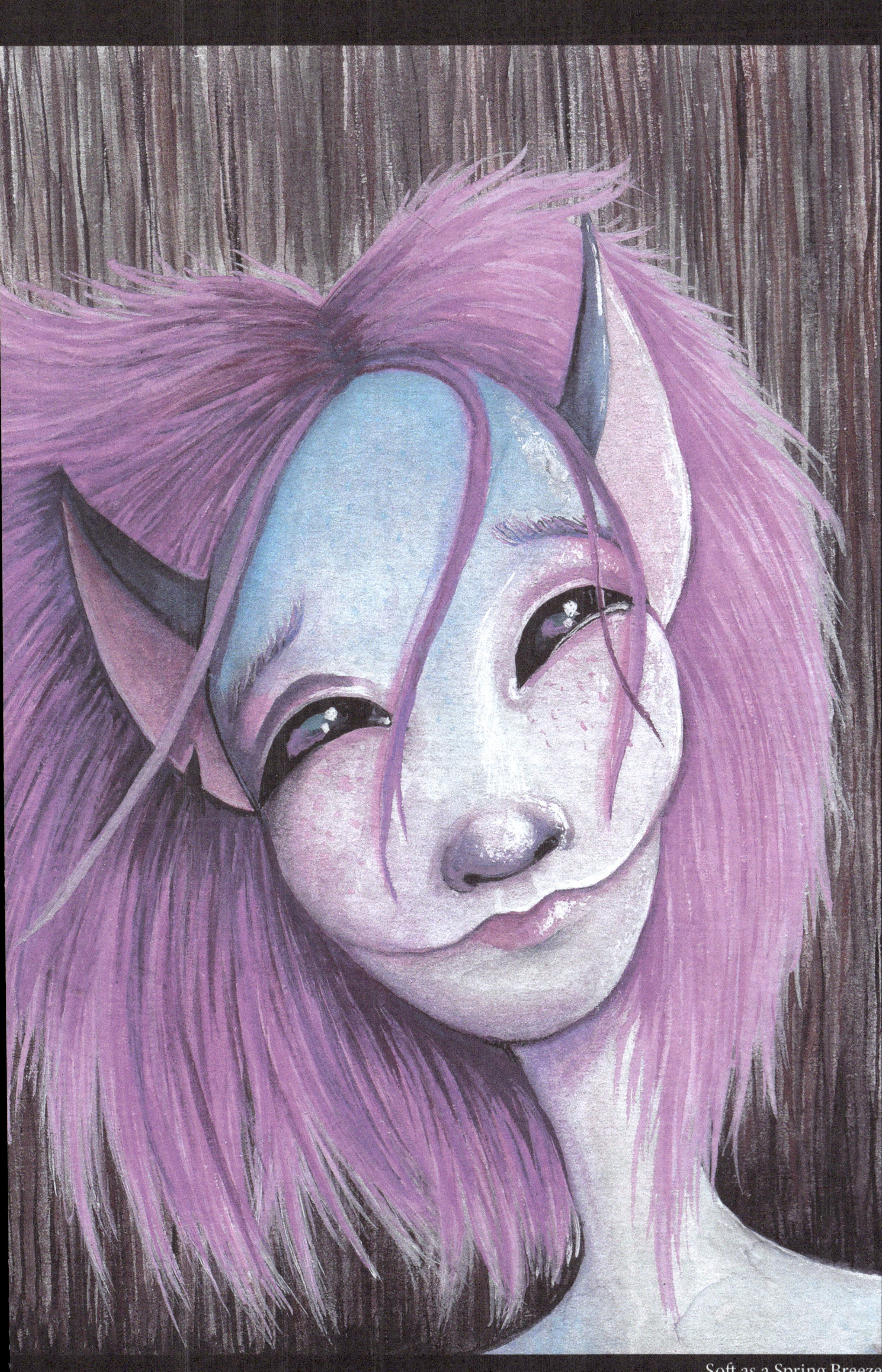

Soft as a Spring Breeze

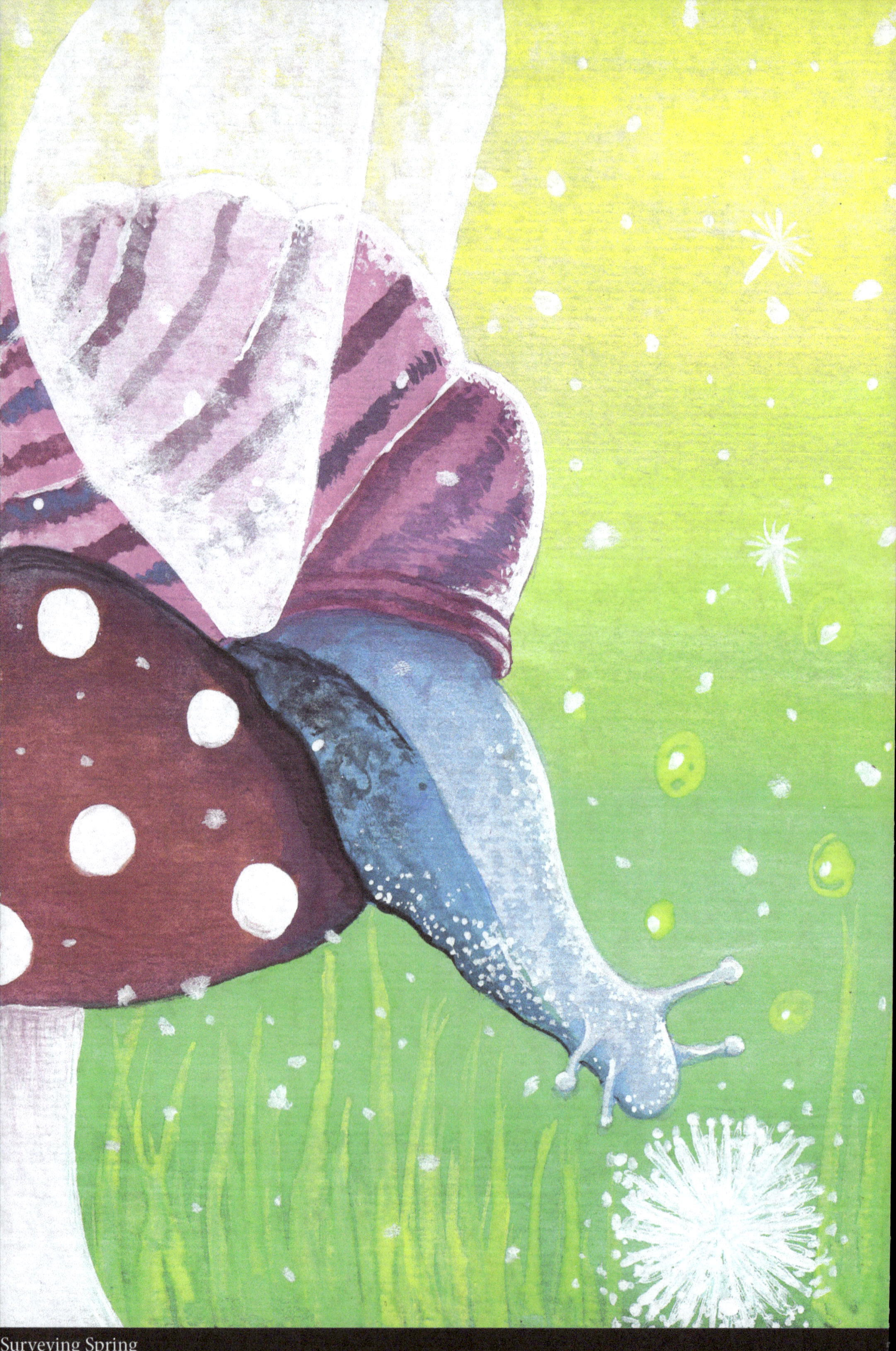

Surveying Spring

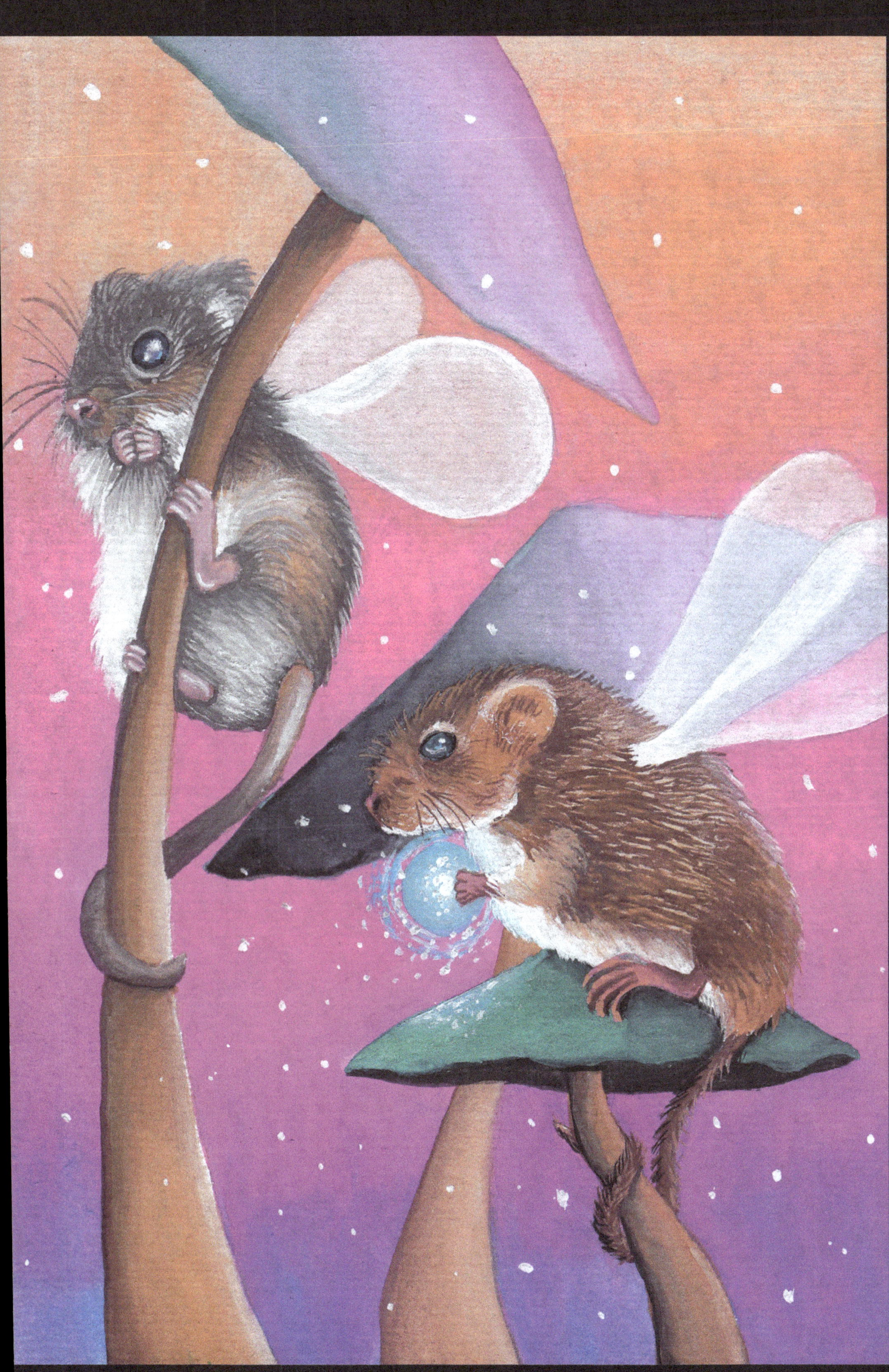

Magical Mice

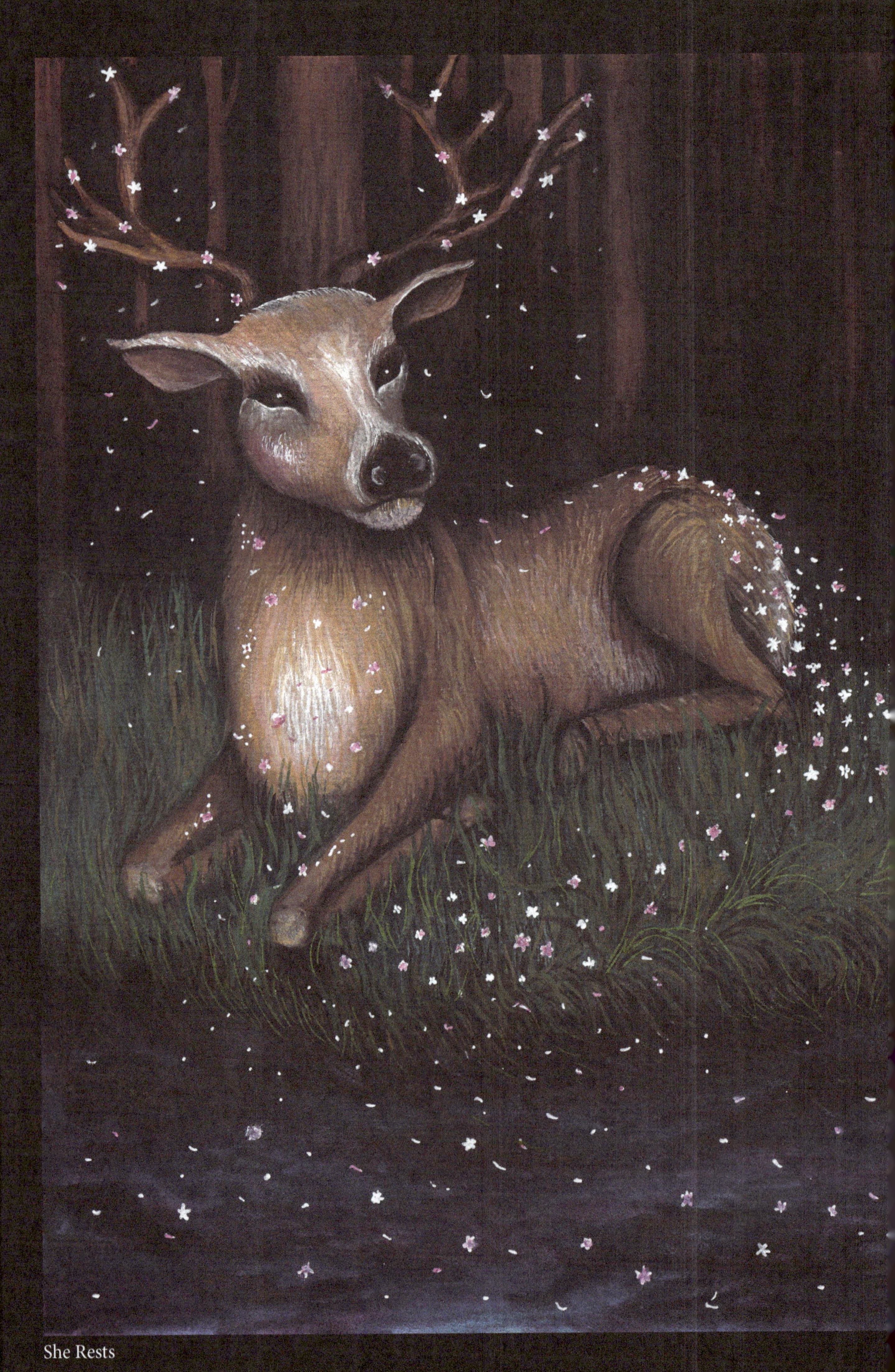

She Rests

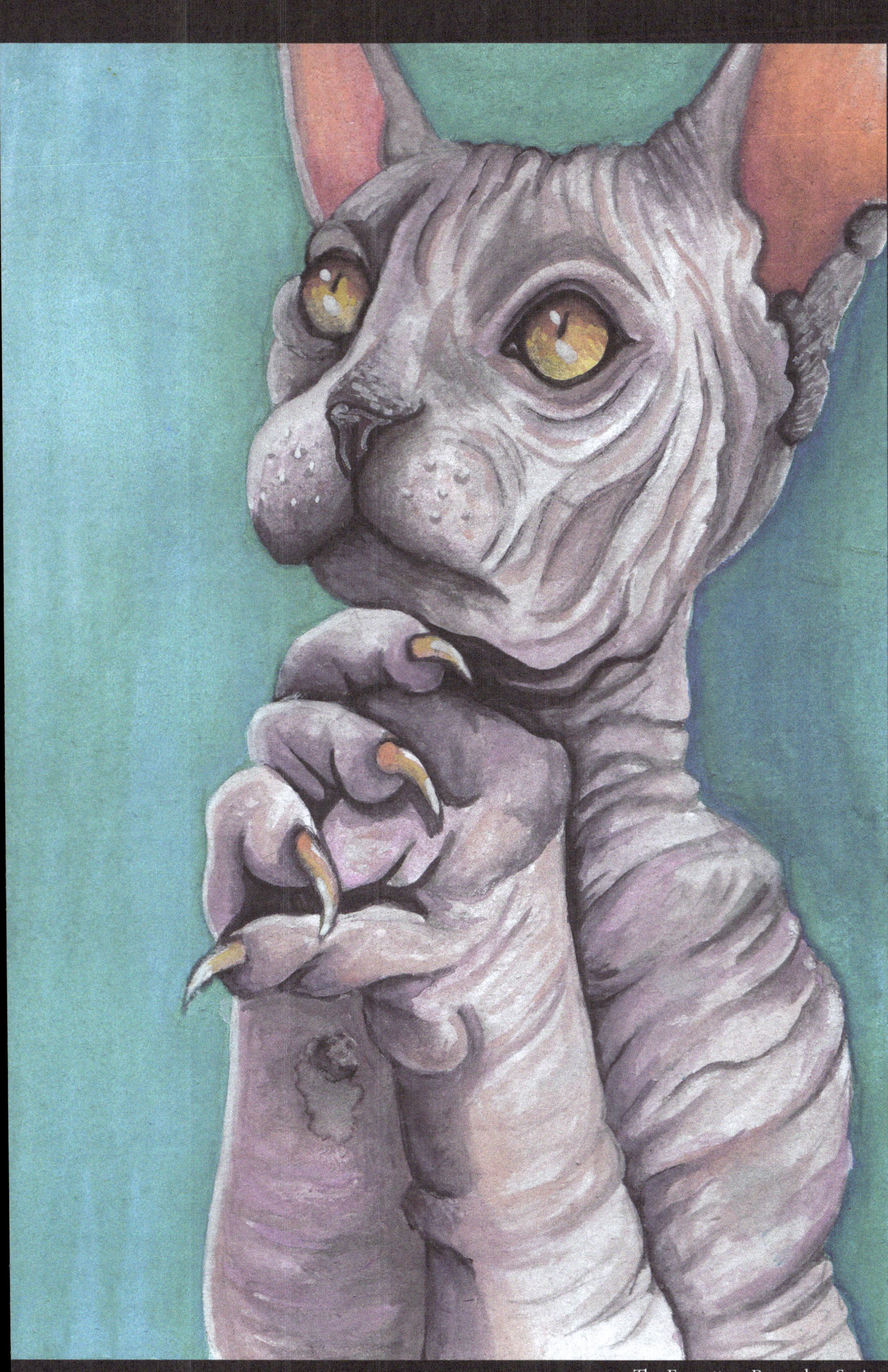

The Forgotten Beseeches Spring

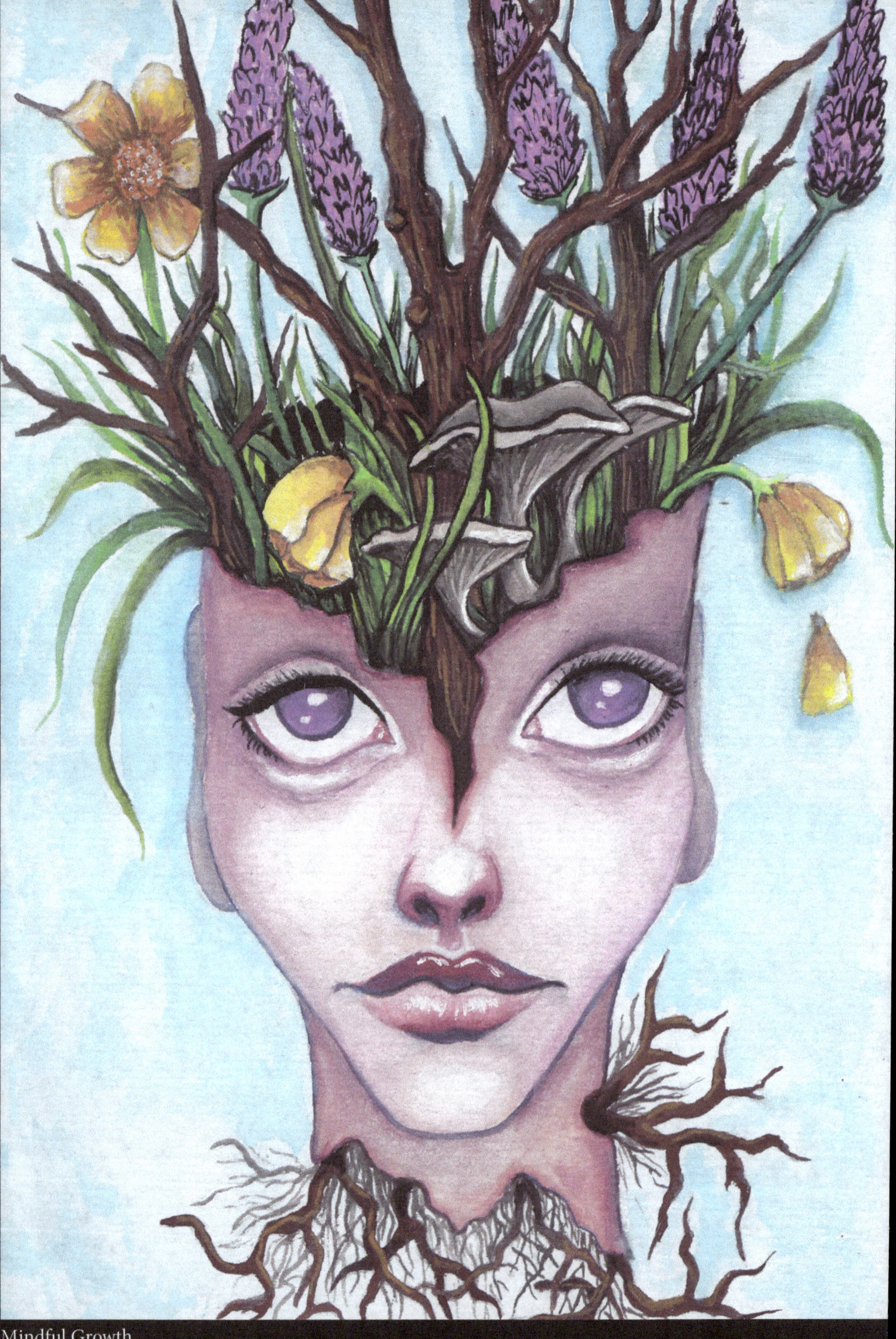

Mindful Growth

And the Seasons continue...

Prints and Merchandise are available instore at
www.sabrinargraven.com